OG MANDINO

THE GREATEST SALESMAN IN THE WORLD

PART II
THE END OF THE STORY

Featuring
The Ten Vows of Success

BANTAM BOOKS
NEW YORK · TORONTO · LONDON · SYDNEY · AUCKLAND

THE GREATEST SALESMAN IN THE WORLD, PART II

A Bantam Book
Bantam hardcover edition/March 1988
Five printings through March 1988
Bantam paperback edition/April 1989

Library of Congress Cataloging-in-Publication Data

Mandino, Og.
  The greatest salesman in the world.

  Contents: —pt. 2. The end of the story.
  1. Success.   I. Title.
BJ1611.2.M32   1988   813'.54   87-47795
                 ISBN 0-553-27699-9

Published simultaneously in the United States and Canada

Bantam Books are published by Bantam Books, a division of Bantam
Doubleday Dell Publishing Group, Inc. Its trademark, consisting of the
words "Bantam Books" and the portrayal of a rooster, is Registered in
U.S. Patent and Trademark Office and in other countries. Marca
Registrada. Bantam Books, 666 Fifth Avenue, New York, New York 10103.

PRINTED IN THE UNITED STATES OF AMERICA

KR   0 9 8 7 6 5 4 3 2

The Greatest Salesman in the World
Part II
The End of the Story

"The most important book of our generation. Og Mandino—the dean of personal enrichment—has created a flawless, priceless masterpiece that will ignite the spirits of millions and live on as an eternal candle to light our way. . . . I vow to internalize and live *the ten vows of success.*"

—DENIS WAITLEY, author, *Seeds of Greatness* and
Being the Best

"Og Mandino has written another timeless classic which deserves our thoughtful reading."

—SPENCER JOHNSON, M.D., author,
The One Minute Manager

"In this wonderful book Og Mandino has produced another masterpiece which will enhance the lives of thousands."

—NORMAN VINCENT PEALE

"This book spans centuries. Yet, in an hour or two, it will influence your life forever—for the better."

—RICHARD M. DEVOS, President, Amway International

"Among all the glitter and glitz of today's torrent of hip, self-help books, Og Mandino's approach is like pure gold. He has distilled the wisdom of the ages and made it pertinent to our twentieth-century lives. Another 'winner'!"

—ART LINKLETTER

For it is written, I will destroy the wisdom of the wise, and will bring to nothing the understanding of the prudent.

What have they, the philosopher, the writer, and the critic of this world to show for all their wisdom? Has not God made the wisdom of this world look foolish?

I Corinthians 1:19–20

A SPECIAL DEDICATION

*H*e was my beloved friend for twelve years and always sat patiently by my side, night after night, whenever I agonized over the shaping of sentences into paragraphs and paragraphs into pages and pages into books.

Very often, late in the evening, he would doze off as I labored over my noisy typewriter but his eyelids never quite closed shut . . . as if he were still standing watch in case I needed him.

I talked out hundreds of writing problems with him, over the years, and he always listened with great patience and understanding. So many character and plot twists came about as a result of my bouncing ideas off him that I'm not certain how I'm ever going to function without him.

His special sofa, near my desk, now seems very large . . . and very empty. I still have to fight back tears whenever I forget and turn to say something to him and then realize that he is not in his favorite spot, nor will he ever be again.

Slippers, you old basset hound, I miss you like hell and if this book ever gets published, plus any others in the future, it will only be because I know you're up there on your own little heavenly sofa, still cheering and barking for your old buddy.

This book, with all my love, is for you, kid. . . .

Og

OG MANDINO
REMEMBERS . . .

*O*ther than Mickey Mantle hitting his five hundredth career home run, Dr. Christiaan Barnard performing the world's first human heart transplant, and Barbra Streisand singing in Central Park, 1967 was not a very good year.

There were race riots in Cleveland, Newark, and Detroit. Israel and Arab nations engaged in a bloody six-day war. The People's Republic of China exploded its first hydrogen bomb. American aircraft bombed Hanoi and three American astronauts were burned to death on their launching pad.

In the midst of all that angst and fear and while the world teetered on the brink of extinction, I enjoyed a great moment of pride that I shall never forget, that fall, when I finally held in my hands the first edition copy of my tiny book, *The Greatest Salesman in the World.*

Being published in such a chaotic year and

against formidable new books by the likes of Gore
Vidal, Isaac Bashevis Singer, Thornton Wilder, Wil-
liam Golding, and Leon Uris did not bode well for
my first fictional effort. My parable about a camel
boy in the time of Christ, an unlikely category in
any era, appeared destined to suffer the same
oblivion as most of the thousands of other new
books being introduced that fall despite publisher
Frederick Fell's heroic efforts to publicize what he
insisted was one of the most important books he
had published in twenty-five years.

And then a miracle happened. Actually, two
miracles. Insurance pioneer, W. Clement Stone, to
whom I had dedicated the book in gratitude for
his help and friendship, was so touched by the
story that he ordered ten thousand copies of *The
Greatest Salesman in the World* for distribution to
every employee and shareholder of his huge Com-
bined Insurance Company. At the same time, Rich
DeVos, co-founder of Amway International, began advising his thousands of distributors, in
speeches across the country, that they should learn
and apply the principles of success found in Og
Mandino's book.

Those two influential leaders planted their
seeds well. Sparked by a growing band of readers
who spontaneously contributed one of the most
extensive word-of-mouth campaigns in publishing
history, sales of the book increased each year to
my great delight and amazement. By 1973 it had
registered an almost unheard of thirty-six printings, sold more than 400,000 hardcover copies,

and was being acclaimed by Paul Nathan of *Publishers Weekly* as "the best-seller that nobody knows." Not once had it appeared on any national best-seller list until Bantam Books acquired the paperback rights, promoted it nationally, and published its first edition in 1974.

I am constantly touched by the wide spectrum of readers who have been influenced by my tale of how ten scrolls of success and happiness came into the possession of a courageous camel boy after he had made an accidental visit to a stable in Bethlehem, one evening. Prison convicts have written that they have memorized every word contained in their battered copies of *Salesman*, drug and alcohol withdrawal patients have admitted sleeping with their book under their pillows, *Fortune* 500 chief executive officers have distributed copies by the thousands to their subordinates while superstars such as Johnny Cash and Michael Jackson continue to sing its praise.

For someone who never imagined anyone would read his effort at writing, except perhaps his immediate family, it is difficult to comprehend that *The Greatest Salesman in the World* has now sold more than 9 million copies in seventeen languages and it has now become the all-time best-selling book for salespeople in the entire world.

Through the years, my mail has often contained the suggestion that I should consider writing a sequel to my two-decade best-seller since, unlike my famous fictional creation, I have not retired. In the years since *Salesman* first saw the light of day, I have managed to produce twelve other books and I also continue to dash around the world giving speeches to large audiences of friends of *Greatest Salesman* on the subject of success.

At first I was completely negative toward the idea of bringing my salesman back for an encore. Writing that book changed my life and that of my family forever and I didn't want to risk producing any sort of sequel that might dilute or harm the original in any way. Also, since I assumed that twenty years must have elapsed for my fictional hero, Hafid, as it had for me in real life, he would be at least age sixty in any sequel and I wasn't certain how much I could do with an old boy like that. Then, one morning, while flying to Lisbon to keynote the North American Company's annual gathering of its top producers, I suddenly realized that I'm a couple of years older than Hafid and here I am still writing and flying around the world giving talks and doing media interviews on radio and television, not to mention that I can still hit a golf ball over 250 yards. If I could still work and perform, so could he! That's when I decided that the greatest salesman in the world should come out of retirement.

Whether you are an old friend of Hafid's or this is your initial contact, I welcome you with love. Read and enjoy . . . and may the words and ideas you find here lighten your load and brighten your path as well as its predecessor has apparently done for so many.

Scottsdale, Arizona

I

On the outskirts of Damascus, in a stately palace of burnished marble framed by giant palm trees, there lived a very special man whose name was Hafid. Now retired, his vast trade empire had once known no boundaries, extending across so many lands from Parthia to Rome to Britannia that he was acclaimed everywhere as the greatest salesman in the world.

By the time he had removed himself from the world of commerce, following his twenty-sixth year of record growth and profit, the inspiring story of Hafid's rise from a lowly camel boy to his mighty position of power and wealth had spread throughout the civilized world.

In those times of great turmoil and upheaval, while almost all of the civilized world bowed meekly to Caesar and his armies, Hafid's fame and reputation had almost elevated him to the status of a living legend. Especially among the poor and downtrodden of Palestine, a border region on the eastern frontier of the empire, Hafid of Damascus was honored in song and poetry as a shining example of how much it was possible to accomplish with one's life despite obstacles and handicaps.

And yet, for a man who had fashioned such a monumental legacy and accumulated a fortune of several million gold talents, the greatest salesman in the world was far from happy in his retirement.

As he had done on so many other days stretching back through the years, Hafid emerged from the rear entrance of his mansion at dawn one morning, treading carefully on the dew-moistened tiles of polished basalt as he headed resolutely across the huge and shadowy courtyard. Far off, a solitary cock crowed as the sun's first rays of silver and gold radiated above the desert from the east.

Hafid paused near the octagonal fountain in the center of the wide patio and inhaled deeply, nodding in appreciation at the thick covering of pale yellow jasmine blossoms clinging to the high stone walls that surrounded his estate. He tightened the girdle of leather at his waist, tugged at his soft linen tunic, and continued at a slower pace until he had passed beneath a natural arcade of cypress boughs and was standing before an elevated granite tomb that was free of all ornamentation.

"Good morning, my beloved Lisha," he half-whispered, reaching forward and softly caressing a white rosebud extending from a single tall bush that guarded the vault's heavy bronze door. Then he retreated to his nearby bench of carved mahogany and sat staring at the crypt that contained the remains of the loving woman who had shared his life, his struggles, and his triumphs.

Hafid felt the pressure of a hand on his shoulder and heard the familiar and hoarse voice of his longtime bookkeeper and faithful companion, Erasmus, even before he opened his eyes.

"Forgive me, master . . . "

"Good morning, old friend."

Erasmus smiled, pointing up at the sun that was now directly above their heads. "Morning has already departed, master. Good afternoon."

Hafid sighed and shook his head. "Another peril of old age. One never sleeps at night, always arises before dawn, and then slumbers like a kitten through the entire day. There is no logic to that. None."

Erasmus nodded and folded his arms, expecting to hear another lecture on the sorrows of growing old. But this was not to be like every other morning, for Hafid had suddenly leaped to his feet and raced toward the tomb in long strides until his hand was on the stone. Then he turned and in a strong voice exclaimed, "I have become a sorry excuse for a human being! Tell me, Erasmus, how long has it been, now, since I began this selfish and isolated life devoted only to feeling sorry for myself?"

Erasmus stared wide-eyed and then replied,

"The great change in thee commenced with the passing of Lisha and your sudden decision to dispose of all your emporiums and caravans, following her entombment. Fourteen years have run their course since you decided to turn your back on the world."

Hafid's eyes had become moist. "Precious ally and brother, how have you managed to tolerate my miserable behavior for so long?"

The old bookkeeper stared down at his hands. "We have been together for almost forty years and my love for you is unconditional. I served you during your greatest moments of success and happiness and I serve you now, just as willingly, even though I have agonized at the living death you seem to have willed for yourself. You cannot return Lisha to life and so you have been trying to join her in that tomb. Remember when you instructed me, many years ago, to secure a red rosebush and plant it next to this white one, after you were dead and laid to rest there?"

"Yes," replied Hafid, "and let us not forget my constant reminders that this palace and warehouse would be yours upon my death. A small recompense for your countless years of loyalty and friendship and all that you have endured from me since we lost Lisha."

Hafid reached out, snapped the stem of the solitary white rosebud, and carried it back to the bench where he placed it carefully in his old friend's lap. "Self-pity is the most terrible of diseases, Erasmus, and I have been afflicted far too long. I have foolishly divorced myself from all humanity, because of my great grief, and made myself a hermit in that mausoleum where you and I reside. Enough! It is time for change!"

"But they have not been wasted years, master. Thy great charitable contributions to the underprivileged of Damascus . . . "

Hafid interrupted. "Money? What sacrifice was that for me? All people of wealth salve their conscience with gifts of gold for the poor. The rich feed off these contributions as much as the hungry and they make certain that the world is made aware of their great generosity which, to them, is no more than a handful of pennies. No, dear friend, applaud not my charity. Instead, sympathize with my unwillingness to share more of myself. . . . "

"And yet," protested Erasmus, "thy seclusion accomplished some good, sire. Have ye not filled thy library with the works of the world's great minds and devoted countless hours to the study of their ideas and principles?"

Hafid nodded. "I have made every attempt to occupy the long days and nights by giving myself the education I never received as a youth and the effort has opened my eyes to a world of wonder and promise that I had little time to appreciate in my pursuit after gold and success. Still, I have prolonged my grief far too long. This world has provided me with everything a man could desire. It is time I began to repay my debt by doing all I can to help make a better life for all mankind. I am not yet ready for my final resting place and the red rose I instructed that you plant here, upon my death, next to this white one that was Lisha's favorite, must wait."

Tears of joy were now flowing down the wrinkled cheeks of Erasmus as Hafid continued. "Livy was writing his history of Rome when he was seventy-five and Tiberius ruled the empire until almost eighty. Compared to them I am only a child . . . a healthy child of sixty! My lungs are clear, my flesh is firm, my vision is excellent, my heart is strong, and my mind is as alert as it was at twenty. I believe I am prepared for a second life . . . !"

"This is such a great miracle!" Erasmus cried, looking toward the heavens. "After years of silent anguish and grief over thy condition, my prayers have finally been answered. Tell me, sire, what has caused this surprise resurrection of the man who was so loved and respected by the world?"

Hafid smiled. "Lisha."

"Lisha?"

"Remember how many times, through the years, what Lisha dreamed would eventually come to pass?"

Erasmus nodded. "The information she provided us, upon awakening, often prevented us from entering into business arrangements that would have cost many fortunes."

Hafid pointed toward the bench. "This morning, as I slumbered here, I dreamed of Lisha. She was holding my hand and walking me through

the streets of Damascus, pointing out how many
in the multitude seemed to be hungry or sick or
hurt or lost or poor or unhappy. I heard her voice,
softly telling me that I could not, any longer,
ignore these people. She reminded me that there
were legions such as these, throughout the world,
who had no one to turn to and I must not shut my
eyes to their plight, burrow a hole in the ground
and hide like a worm."

"Lisha was never known to speak to you in
such a manner, sire."

"Correction, Erasmus. She had no cause to
do so in the old days. But wait, there is more to
my dream. She then told me that my life was
about to begin again and warned me that my days
as a recluse were over because a stranger would
come to my door, this very day, and I was not to
turn him away as I had done to so many in the
past. This stranger, Lisha said, would provide me
with the key to unlock my future, a future that
would affect many lives. Erasmus? Erasmus, why
are you so pale? What is wrong?"

"I beg your forgiveness, sire, but in my great
joy at this surprising transformation in thee, I
neglected to announce that there is a visitor awaiting thy pleasure in the library."

"A friend?"

"A stranger, at least to me. He said his name
is Galenus, he is from Jerusalem, and he has a
business proposition for you."

"Why was he not sent away, as you have

done to all visitors according to my orders, for these many years?"

"There was something special about this man, sire, and I could not bring myself to request that he leave."

"Does he not know that my days of hearing business propositions have long passed?"

Erasmus smiled and cocked his head slyly. "He does not. Nor does he know that his presence has already been announced in a dream. Is it still thy wish that I send him on his way?"

Hafid's laughter echoed throughout the courtyard for the first time in more than a decade as the two old friends embraced and turned toward the palace.

"Let us hurry, Erasmus. One must never keep a dream waiting."

II

*T*he stranger was standing near the goldfish pond in the center of the vast library, gazing in awe at the thousands of parchment rolls stored neatly on shelves of walnut that extended from a dark marble floor to a high ceiling enhanced by mosaic tiles of blue and gold.

Galenus was short and his closely cropped white hair provided strong contrast to his dark features. Despite his lack of stature, there was an authority about the man hinting that here was one who demanded and received respect. Erasmus stepped back after introducing the visitor to his master.

"I am most honored to meet, at long last, the greatest salesman in the world," Galenus said, bowing at the waist. "And I am overwhelmed by this room. What a magnificent collection! Even Emperor Claudius would turn green with envy."

Hafid nodded proudly. "Yes, here I am able to consult with Horace and Virgil and Catullus and Lucretius and scores of others who have been blessed with great vision and wisdom. And on that south wall is perhaps the only complete collection of Varro's works . . . six hundred and twenty volumes in seventy-four books. However, I doubt that you have come here to discuss my collection and I apologize for keeping you waiting so long. Let us sit here," he said, pointing to a couch whose back was inlaid with tortoiseshell and gems.

Taking his cue from Hafid's stern tone, Galenus came swiftly to the purpose of his visit. "Sir, I have been given to understand that because of the immense trade empire you once controlled, you have the ability to speak with eloquence in the tongue of the Jew, the Greek, and the Roman. Is that correct?"

Hafid frowned and glanced toward Erasmus who shrugged his shoulders and looked away. "I doubt that there is very much eloquence in my words," he replied, "but I have trained myself to at least communicate in all three languages."

Galenus leaned toward his host. "Most honored merchant, we are entering an era where mankind's thirst for knowledge seems to know no bounds. A revolution of the mind and the spirit is taking place led by the common man who is no longer content to remain common. He seeks guidance, counsel, and teaching on how he can improve his lot in life through wiser application of the talents he has possessed since birth. To satisfy this mass migration into the world of self-improvement, thousands of teachers and orators now travel from city to city, sharing their knowledge and experience on every possible subject . . . from astrology to farming to investing to medicine, lecturing to huge crowds, both schooled and unschooled, on hillsides, in gymnasiums, forums, theaters, and even temples."

Galenus paused for some response from his host but when Hafid remained silent, he continued. "Of course, among this legion of lecturers there are charlatans with silver tongues who dispense useless information and whose message is of little value compared to the high admission fee they charge. On the other hand, there are many powerful masters of oratory in the tradition of the Romans, Cato and Cicero, who draw from a lifetime of struggles and observations and leave their audiences with valuable lessons and techniques that will enhance any life. Many who tour have built great followings and earn immense fortunes on the platform."

Hafid raised his hand, a patient smile on his lips. "I am well aware, sir, of these masters in the art of rhetoric. Except for the few who stir up trouble, I applaud their efforts to make this a better world for all. But what is all that to me?"

"Great salesman," said Galenus, "I am an experienced promoter of exhibitions, games, and other events of entertainment for the masses. In the past twenty years I have produced and staged debates, lectures, concerts, prize fights, wrestling matches, plays, and countless races by foot and chariot. I have made presentations in Athens, Jerusalem, Alexandria, Rome, and hundreds of smaller cities and towns throughout the civilized world."

"That is indeed interesting, Galenus, and I am impressed. But why are you here?"

There was a slight tremor in the visitor's voice. "Sir, I would like to represent the greatest salesman in the world on several speaking tours. I am certain that with your background you must have a message of hope and success that could change many lives and after hearing your powerful voice I know that you could deliver it with great authority. Since your reputation would guarantee huge crowds everywhere, I want to place you on the platforms and stages of this world so that you may have the opportunity to instruct and inspire the common man and woman in the techniques necessary to make at least some of his or her dreams come true. The world is sorely in need of your expert guidance, Hafid."

It required several minutes before Galenus recovered from the shock of Hafid instantly accepting his proposal. After lunch, during which Hafid related his strange dream of the morning and Lisha's prediction, the two continued their discussion at the large teak table in the library while Erasmus made many notes.

"Our first tour," Galenus explained, "would be a brief but important learning experience for you as you work at refining your talk and acquiring some of the fundamentals of good oratory by practicing before small audiences. I shall monitor your first few speeches and make any suggestions I believe might improve your delivery. Working in nearby towns and villages will also serve as a testing period for you and the initial four or five lectures should be sufficient to help you decide whether or not you want to continue on to the capitals of the world where the crowds would number in the thousands instead of the hundreds."

"That is very considerate of you," smiled Hafid. "If I am going to make a fool of myself, it is well that only a few bear witness to my failure."

Galenus laughed. "I do not believe that will happen. With your permission I shall depart in the morning and commence making all necessary arrangements for your appearances in four or five locations, none spaced more than a half day's journey from the next. Then I shall return and accompany you through the entire tour. Can I assume that the man whose caravans covered the world still has, in his stables, a sturdy closed carriage large enough to transport us and our personal effects with some degree of comfort?"

"I have a favorite vehicle that may need some restoration after sitting idle for so many years. Erasmus, of course, will also accompany us. This carriage is large enough to sleep four and requires a four-horse pull; however, I have several Arabian grays who can come out of retirement with their master. The carriage was a gift from the governor of Judea, Pontius Pilate, at least fifteen years ago after I gave him a good price on two hundred prize stallions for his cavalry stationed at Caesarea."

"Excellent. In each town I shall rent the most appropriate forum for your lecture, whether it be a theater, gymnasium, arena, or school and I shall recruit those local people needed to best promote your appearance to the public."

Erasmus finally ended his long silence. "Galenus, you mentioned the great wealth accumulated by some traveling orators and I have been patiently waiting for you to describe the financial arrangements you propose for this venture."

"Of course. All expenses such as food, lodging, rental of the lecture facility, stable, and payments to those in each town who promote our programs are first deducted from the total of monies collected for admissions. Then I retain twenty-five percent of the balance as my fee and remit the remainder to Hafid. This is the standard percentage charged by the most respected of our profession."

"That seems to be most fair and equitable," said Hafid. "Turn over all my earnings to Erasmus. He has guarded my purse strings for many years and I see no reason to change our habits at this late date. Later, we can decide what charities should benefit."

Galenus said, "I shall be gone for at least two weeks, arranging your itinerary. While I am away you will have time to prepare your lecture and rehearse its delivery. Actually, the great orators I have met tell me that they are always practicing

. . . that every lecture is a rehearsal for the next one . . . and that the words they use always seem to change to fit their audience, the important news of the moment, and even the weather."

Hafid was now scribbling on a small piece of parchment. "In length of time, Galenus, how long should the lecture be?"

"There is no prescribed length. I am familiar with a famous philosopher who has been known to orate for four or more hours and say little and yet I still recall, years ago, hearing a young preacher on a mountain near Jerusalem who touched every listener present with his power and his love in a discourse of less than half an hour. I suggest that you write a speech you can deliver in an hour's time and then memorize enough of it so that your delivery seems natural without your having to read any of it. Beyond an hour, even the most loyal of audiences begin to suffer from a terrible numbing sensation in their lower posteriors."

Erasmus glanced apprehensively at his master. "Dost thou have any idea, at this early time, what will be the subject of your lectures to the people?"

Hafid rose and began pacing the tiled floor as if he were already rehearsing. "I have often thought of those meetings in years long past when all our managers gathered here, in this very room, to review with me the results of the past year and their future goals. I always spoke to them, not of the quality of our goods or the sales volume achieved, but rather of each person's vision of the future and how much control it was possible to exercise over the year to come through the better use of his talent and potential. I talked often of change and how it is painful but necessary, reminding my people that we are always growing, no matter what our age, unlike the lilies of the field that bloom, turn to straw, and are plowed under or blow away. And I was forever reminding them of the great wonders they could perform providing they learned to stand guard, night and day, against the worst enemy they would ever have . . . themselves. One has only to walk down any street in Damascus or any other city, today, to bear witness to how many have lost their way. Lisha, bless her soul, showed me in my dream this morning. And I know from my own observations that this is not a happy world. Ten shed tears for every one who smiles. Something is wrong, very wrong. God provided us with all the tools necessary to achieve any goal but we have lost the plans and drawings and so we build nothing but houses of sorrow. Perhaps, in my small way, I can assist God . . . by dropping a few pebbles to mark a path for those who seek guidance, just as my path was guided, long ago, by another."

III

And so it came to pass that at an age when most would be content to sit in the shade with their memories, the greatest salesman in the world embarked on a new career.

His initial speech was presented in a musty meeting hall on the outskirts of Caesarea Philippi to an audience of less than one hundred. Afterwards, over supper in a nearby caravan stop, Hafid reviewed the evening with his two companions.

"Your message," said Galenus, "was both powerful and simple and I am certain that the many principles of success you presented were of great value to everyone in attendance, no matter what his or her condition might be. And, of course, no one on any platform is able to speak from your position because no one alive has achieved your success! My heart flutters with anticipation when I consider your appearances, later, in the world's great cities such as Rome and Jerusalem. It will be

necessary for you to speak on many evenings, no
matter how large the forums, before we will have
satisfied the immense crowds who will gather to
learn from the master. What a pleasant thought!"

Hafid pushed aside his plate, unsmiling, and
said, "Kindly withhold thy compliments, Galenus,
until I have truly earned them. For now, just tell
me how I can improve on my weak performance
of this evening."

"This was only your first presentation, Hafid,
and ye must not be too harsh on thyself. The art
of oratory is a skill not easily acquired. Tonight I
noticed that you had forgotten several points you
had planned to make in your speech but you
continued on so calmly that I doubt anyone in the
room realized your error. Perhaps you might wish
to consider employing more body movement during your delivery. Now and then walk closer to
your audience, pause, and then just turn and walk
away from them without saying anything. Remember that a good speaker is, first of all, a good
actor. Gesture with your arms whenever you wish
to emphasize a point and also raise and lower
your voice. Most important, work at looking into
the eyes of as many in your audience as you can,
one person at a time, just as if you were having
private conversations with each despite the distance between you."

Hafid shook his head sadly. "I have much to
learn."

Galenus patted his arm. "Patience, my friend,
patience. I know that you did not become the

great salesman that you are in a day. Over the years I have handled hundreds of performers and I must tell you that I was amazed, this evening, at your poise and self-control. But in retrospect I should not have been surprised. After all the challenges you have met and overcome in your lifetime, tonight was probably of little concern to thee."

"On the contrary," sighed Hafid, "I'm not certain that my message had any value to those people. They seemed unmoved by my words and there was little applause at the conclusion."

"It will come, sire," assured Erasmus, "it will come."

But it did not come. Not in Bethsaida nor Chorazin nor Capernaum was Hafid able to ignite his audiences.

His final scheduled appearance on this initial tour was in the hillside village of Nazareth and since this was a crossroads for both military and commercial travel, Galenus and his helpers had managed to crowd nearly three hundred into the dining hall of the town's only inn.

Hafid, in later years, was quick to acknowledge that his decision to speak at Nazareth had a great influence on the remainder of his life. After the sorry evening in Capernaum, when he was certain he had failed his audience of fishermen and merchants, he almost canceled the final scheduled stop and returned to Damascus. Only his habit of never giving up on anything he had begun and his inability to ever mouth the words "I quit," pushed him on to Nazareth.

Although Hafid's delivery had improved with each presentation, the Nazareth speech, itself, was not memorable. However, sitting in the second row of benches, listening attentively to every word, was an old and respected friend, Sergius Paulus, longtime Roman governor of the island of Cyprus, who smiled and nodded encouragingly throughout the speech and was on his feet, applauding loudly, as soon as Hafid had delivered his closing remarks.

After Hafid had responded to the final question from his audience, the two old friends ascended the stairway of the inn, arm in arm, followed by Galenus and Erasmus. Sergius lit oil lamps in the dark room before beckoning his guests to enter.

"This is not quite comparable to any of the rooms in my palace in Paphos," he smiled as he embraced Hafid again, "but just seeing you, great salesman, and your trusted comrade, Erasmus, is sufficient luxury for me. How long has it been?" he asked as he poured wine from a large leather flask into four goblets.

"Nearly twenty years, governor, but ye have not aged a single day."

"Ah ha, even the greatest salesman sometimes strains at the truth," Sergius replied and while they sipped their wine Erasmus recounted to Galenus the many happy and profitable years of trade that had taken place between the caravans of Hafid and the people of Cyprus.

Finally, Hafid asked the question that had been on his mind since he had first glimpsed Sergius in the audience. What was the esteemed governor of the island of Cyprus doing so far from his territory and why was he in such a forlorn little village as Nazareth?

"In a way, Hafid, you are to blame for my being here. Does the name Saul or Paul of Tarsus mean anything to you?"

"Of course. A little preacher with a big voice. He was trying to sell a new religion to the people based on the teachings of a man called Jesus who had been crucified by Pontius Pilate for sedition against Rome. I met Paul when everyone had turned against him and his life was in danger. He came to me, he claimed, after hearing a voice while praying in the Jewish temple in Jerusalem. That voice had told him that if he wanted to sell his beliefs to others he should learn how to do so from the greatest salesman in the world."

"And you agreed to help him?"

"Yes."

Sergius nodded and smiled. "You must have provided excellent training. Paul had the courage to come to Cyprus and ask for an audience with me, on the strength of his friendship with you. Two days later he had converted me to his faith. I have been a follower of Jesus ever since."

"You? A Roman?"

"Yes. I may be the first for all I know. Did not

the little man try to convert you after you had
provided him with such valuable advice on selling
ideas as easily as merchandise?"

"No. He departed that same night and I have
never seen him since although he has written to
me often, through the years. But you still haven't
explained, Sergius, why you are here in this God-
forsaken place."

The governor laughed. "God-forsaken? Hardly.
I finally decided that my hourglass of life is almost
filled and I wanted to walk in the footsteps of
Jesus, here in Palestine, before I die. I left the
government of Cyprus in able hands and have
taken a three-month leave in order to see what I
could of the world where Jesus lived and touched
so many lives."

"But of what significance is Nazareth?"

"Jesus spent his youth and grew to manhood
here, assisting his father in a small carpenter
shop. . . ."

"But he was not born here," interrupted Hafid.

Sergius paled. "How do you know that if you
are not a follower?"

"Because I was with the infant Jesus, soon
after his birth, in a stable in Bethlehem."

Shocked at what he had heard, Sergius placed
both his hands on his mouth and waited for Hafid
to continue.

"I was a camel boy for the great caravan of
Pathros but had spent three difficult days in Beth-
lehem trying to sell a single seamless red robe that
Pathros had challenged me to sell in order to

prove that I should be promoted from camel boy to salesman. By the evening of the third day, after failing to sell the garment hundreds of times, I ate some bread in the inn and then went behind that building to a cave where my animal was tied. Because of the chill in the air I had decided to sleep on the hay, next to my beloved donkey, rather than ride into the hills. After a good night's rest I would be prepared, on the morrow, to exert supreme effort to sell the robe and I was certain I would finally succeed. But when I entered the stable I came upon a young man and woman sitting close to a single candle and at their feet was the open box that usually held cattle fodder. In that manger was an infant sleeping on some straw and I could see that the baby had little protection from the cold except the tattered cloaks of the mother and father that covered him."

"What did you do?"

Hafid clenched his hands together and inhaled deeply. "I agonized for several moments, picturing all the terrible consequences of my returning to the caravan without the robe, or coins from its sale. Finally I removed it from the back of my animal and wrapped it carefully around the baby after handing the worn garments back to a shocked mother and father. You know, Sergius, it was almost fifty years ago and yet I can still see that lovely young mother sobbing with gratitude as she came close and kissed my cheek."

Hafid stood and began pacing back and forth, his hands behind his back while his audience of

three listened attentively. "I rode back to the caravan a broken child. I had failed in my mission and
now I was certain that I would be a shoveler of
camel dung forever. Head bowed, in total defeat,
I failed even to notice the bright star that had
followed me all the way from Bethlehem back to
the campsite of the caravan but Pathros, my master, did. He was waiting for me, despite the late
hour, at the edge of our row of tents, pointing up
at the brightly lit sky and asking me what wondrous deed I had been a part of, and I told him
none. However, he looked upon the bright star as
a special sign from God and passed on to me the
ten scrolls of success that I used, throughout my
days, to achieve more of the good things of this
life than any person deserves. Furthermore, I was
commanded by Pathros not to share the scrolls
with anyone until someday, he said, when I would
be given a special sign from the person who was
next to receive the scrolls, even though it was
possible that person would not realize that he or
she was presenting a sign to me."

Sergius smiled. "And the person who eventually received the scrolls from you was Paul?"

"It was. Three years after I had disbanded my
trade empire. By then I had almost despaired of
ever passing them on to anyone."

"How did you know it was Paul who was to
receive the scrolls? What was the special sign?"

"In his knapsack was a red seamless robe that
he said was the favorite of Jesus and had been
worn by him throughout his lifetime. There were

dark bloodstains on it from the whippings that Jesus had suffered before he was crucified. To my astonishment, near the hem of the robe I found the familiar mark of the guild that had made these popular robes for Pathros and I also found the mark of Pathros, a circle within a square. Still uncertain of what I was holding in my hands, I asked Paul if he knew any of the circumstances surrounding the birth of Jesus and he then related to me that Jesus had been born in a stable in Bethlehem and above the stable had shone the brightest star that man had ever witnessed. Then I knew that the robe in Paul's possession was the very same robe I had wrapped around the small body of Jesus on that fateful night. That was all the sign I needed. Erasmus, who was present at my meeting with Paul, went to the tower in my palace where the scrolls of success had been stored for safekeeping and we presented them to Paul with our love."

"The wisdom on those scrolls must have been very powerful," said Sergius. "My representatives report that Paul has enjoyed great success winning converts in the cities of Pisidia, Lycaonia, Perga, Antioch, Iconium, Lystra, and countless more."

"I am not surprised," replied Hafid.

Sergius drained his wine goblet and asked, "Where is your next speaking appearance?"

"No more are scheduled for the present. We three shall return to Damascus tomorrow and after a few days we shall meet and attempt to evaluate this entire speaking experience before deciding whether or not there is a future for me on the platform trying to affect people's lives for the better."

"Would you be willing to remain in Nazareth yet another day if I provided you with a strong enough reason?"

Hafid studied the lined face of his friend for several moments before nodding his head.

The old governor grasped both of Hafid's hands and said, "Great salesman, on the morrow you will meet, once again, the woman who kissed the cheek of the young camel boy in that stable, so many years ago!"

IV

*T*he two old friends met on the following morning at Nazareth's only well, located in an open space on the side of the main road near the center of town. Dust filled the air along with hoarse shouts, cries, and laughter as a long line of women and children waited their turn to fill jars and pitchers at the open trough.

Hafid watched with great interest when a huge trade caravan halted near the water supply and several camel boys filled and refilled wide stone casks many times before their thirsty animals were satisfied.

Sergius nudged his friend. "Was that once your chore when you labored in the caravans of Pathros?"

"That was one of my more pleasant duties." Hafid smiled as the smelly animals lumbered past on the narrow cobblestone street.

The two men waited patiently until there was

an open space at the stone tank before they dipped their hands into the cool water and drank. "Jesus and his mother came here daily," Sergius said with reverence.

Hafid smiled sympathetically at his old friend's pious treatment of such a common and dirty public well shared by both human and animal. "And he walked on these cobblestones and breathed this air and played in those fields," he replied in jest, but Sergius did not return his smile.

"Yes," the governor said softly. "He spent nearly thirty years of his life here working at his father's trade with saw and hammer and plane. I have already purchased some furniture from the villagers which they tell me was fashioned by his hands. When I return to Cyprus I shall have a special room prepared for it in the palace."

They had almost reached the open countryside before Sergius finally stopped and pointed to a small square limestone house nearly hidden beneath two pomegranate trees. "That is where Jesus lived most of his life. His carpenter shop is no more than a small room in the rear."

"Perhaps we should not disturb the old woman," Hafid said as Sergius hurried along the weed-strewn path until they were at the front door which was sorely in need of paint.

The governor patted Hafid's arm. "It will be all right. During the past week I have visited with Mary many times and we have become good friends. Early this morning I notified her, by messenger, that I was bringing you today."

Hafid inhaled deeply. "You reminded her of our long-ago meeting in that stable in Bethlehem?"

"Oh no, that would spoil my surprise. I merely sent word that I was bringing an old friend. Your presence will not upset her. She told me that she has become accustomed to strangers, most of them well meaning, who want to see and speak with the mother of Jesus."

"Does she live alone?"

"Yes. She has been a widow for many years and all her children are either dead or living elsewhere. Her son, James, visits her often although his days are filled now that he is head of a new church in Jerusalem."

Sergius had knocked only twice before the door swung open quietly on its old leather hinges. "Peace be to thee, beloved lady," said Sergius as he gently grasped the elderly woman's extended hand and touched it lightly to his lips.

"And to thee, Sergius," she said, smiling warmly at Hafid when he was introduced. She served them tall goblets of goat's milk and cheese and placed a large tray of pomegranates and figs within their reach as they talked of many things concerning the village. Hafid was entranced by Mary's large olive-shaped eyes and her nearly jet black hair although he was certain that she was at least ten years his senior.

Even her voice belied her age. "You spoke last evening at the inn?" she asked as she tilted her head toward Hafid.

"I did but I fear that I was not much of a success."

"How do you know?"

"There was little reaction from the audience. If Sergius, here, had not led the applause I doubt there would have been any."

Mary smiled faintly. "At least they didn't threaten your life. Jesus spoke only once here in Nazareth, in the synagogue as he was trying to decide what course to take with his life following forty days of meditation he had spent in the desert. His words, that Sabbath morning, so infuriated the people that they seized him and led him up to the tallest cliff but before they could cast him to the rocks below, he escaped."

"That I did not know," exclaimed Sergius. "These were the same people who had grown up with him, played with him, attended school with him?"

"The same," said Mary. "Most could not understand why their friend and neighbor, the carpenter, was suddenly speaking as if he had special authority from God. To them this was blasphemy which under our law is punishable by death."

"And that was his first public speech anywhere?"

"It was . . . and for much of that morning I was convinced it would be his last."

Sergius turned to Hafid. "These stories must be preserved but no one, to my knowledge, has written them down as yet. How sad."

The governor redirected his attention toward

Mary, and Hafid watched, entranced, as one of the most powerful officials in the Roman empire addressed the old woman with a tenderness and respect Hafid had never witnessed in Sergius before.

"How did Jesus deal with his frightening reception and treatment?"

"He put it out of his mind and was preaching, on the following Sabbath, in the synagogue of nearby Capernaum. The people there received him with love and attention. Later, when we talked about his terrible experience here, I remember he just smiled and said that he should have known that no prophet hath any honor in his own country."

Sergius tilted his head back and closed his eyes. "These stories must be written down, they must!"

Hafid waited until Mary had refilled his glass with cool milk. Then he said, "From what little I know of Jesus, I understand that he never preached outside of Palestine. As his mother you must have had many opportunities to hear your son and his message."

Mary nodded. "In the beginning, as he was building his following and teaching his apostles, I heard him often. But when the Sanhedrin and the Roman governor began to send agents to spy on my son's actions and words, he insisted that I return and remain here, out of harm's way. More than once, whenever he and his people passed through Nazareth, he would sit and hold my hand and try to prepare me for what was to come."

Mary bit on her lower lip and turned her head away. Sergius glanced at Hafid and nodded. Now was the time. The governor leaned forward and placed his hand gently on the woman's back.

"Blessed lady, I have something special to tell you."

"Yes, Sergius."

"This old friend of mine, Hafid, accompanied me here today because he wanted very much to see you again."

"Again?" Mary frowned and cocked her head. "Ever since he walked in that door I was certain that I knew him but when nothing was said I merely considered it a fault of my old age. We have met before, great salesman?"

"Only once, many years ago, Mary."

The mother of Jesus pulled her shawl down around her neck and leaned across the table toward Hafid. Without speaking he leaned closer to her and Mary's hands reached up until they were covering both sides of his face. She ran her fingers down his cheeks and said, "Was it before this lovely beard covered your face?"

"Long before then."

Mary's right thumb softly caressed the deep cleft in Hafid's chin as she stared into his grey eyes that were now moist. Suddenly she turned toward Sergius, mouth ajar, with tears streaming down her wrinkled cheeks and her hands still on the great salesman's face.

"I know him," she sobbed. "I felt something special in his manner since the moment he passed through my doorway. I know him, Sergius! This is another miracle!"

"And who is he?" Sergius smiled lovingly.

Mary drew Hafid's face closer and kissed him gently on the cheek. "He is my little angel on a donkey. In the damp stable in Bethlehem, only a few hours after Jesus was born, he appeared from the shadows and wrapped my baby in a warm red robe. Then he rode off into the night and I never had the opportunity to thank him."

Hafid touched his cheek and said softly. "You did thank me. You kissed me then, as you did now, and my life changed that night."

"And now, perhaps it will change again," she said as she rose and went to a large trunk in the far corner of the room. She removed a leather sack from the box and when she returned to the table she placed the sack in Hafid's arms. "This is yours, precious man. He would have wanted you to have it."

While Sergius Paulus knelt silently near his friend's chair, Hafid slowly withdrew the red robe that had been the favorite of Jesus from the bag. Again he fought back tears as he rubbed his hands gently over the soft red fabric. "The last time I saw this it was in the possession of Paul. He told me that after much searching, in Jerusalem, he found the Roman soldier who had won it in a game of dice after . . . after the . . . crucifixion."

Mary nodded. "Paul returned the robe to me

several years ago. There were bloodstains on one side from the whippings that Jesus received before they killed him and I could not bear looking at them so I soaked it for many hours in a light solution of lye."

Hafid continued to stroke the garment. "What remarkable craftsmanship! Look how the color has not faded and the weave is frayed only along one side after more than fifty years! Amazing!"

"Jesus wore it for all occasions, especially whenever he was to appear before large crowds. He said that next to his prayers, feeling that robe on his shoulders gave him all the confidence he needed to deal with any situation. Perhaps it will do the same for you. Did you not say that there was little reaction, from the crowd, to your words last night?"

Hafid folded the robe and handed it to Mary. "I cannot accept this priceless garment. It should be on display in some great place of worship, for all the world to see, certainly not draped around my undeserving shoulders."

"Please," said Mary, placing her small hand over Hafid's. "Take it . . . and wear it. When Jesus was a child I often told him the story of how another little boy visited him, soon after he was born, and presented him with this robe to keep him warm. It was the best way I knew to teach him the true meaning of love—when one gives all one can give to help another, with no thought of any reward. He learned that lesson well, thanks to you. You cannot believe, great salesman, that just coincidence has reunited you and this robe after all these years. Make an old lady happy and accept it. I have many other possessions of my son to keep me company as well as years of loving memories. At long last the robe has been returned to its rightful owner."

"I shall never forget this day," sobbed Hafid as he raised the red garment and held it softly against his moist cheeks.

V

Both men were silent, deep in their own thoughts, following their departure from the house of Mary. Sergius halted, after they had reached the main road, and turned to his friend.

"I am most grateful for your company this day."

"Say no more," protested the great salesman, holding up the sack that contained the robe of Jesus. "It is my heart that overflows with gratitude."

"Are you tired?"

Hafid shook his head.

"Will they be expecting you back at your elegant wagon soon?"

"No. I told Erasmus that I might be gone the entire day. He and Galenus are probably busy doing their bookkeeping and satisfying all our obligations from last night's speech."

Sergius turned, pointing above his head to a steep hill that rose abruptly above the side of the road to their right. "This is the tallest hill in all of Nazareth, I am told. See that large fig tree on the very top?"

Hafid shaded the sun from his eyes with both hands. "Yes."

"Do you suppose that ancient body of yours might be capable of climbing up there, if I provided some help?"

"Roman arrogance never truly disappears, does it?" muttered Hafid. "If you can manage the ascent, I'm certain that I can also make it . . . and without any assistance. But why should I want to struggle up through fields of thistles and loose stones in order to sit under a miserable uncultivated fig tree when I have several groves of them, both the early and late variety, back in Damascus?"

Sergius grinned. "But not like that one, mighty merchant. Yesterday, after I had visited with Mary, she accompanied me back to the well and when we passed this place she looked up at that solitary tree and told me that it was there that Jesus went, from the time he was very young, whenever he wanted to be alone. See, to our right, the narrow path that leads to the top. I would have gone up yesterday but the sun was already setting when I parted from Mary and furthermore I did not wish to miss your speech. Would ye be willing to climb up there with me now? I understand the view is well worth the struggle to reach the pinnacle."

"Lead the way," Hafid cried out as he hoisted the leather bag to his shoulder and fell in behind Sergius. Both were perspiring and breathing heavily by the time they had reached the summit that was bare of vegetation except for the solitary fig tree and small threads of moss that partially covered the slopes of grey rock. Hafid leaned his sack against the tree trunk before easing his weary body onto the smooth stone surface next to Sergius.

At their feet, far below, lay the village of Nazareth with its straggling houses of white limestone, green meadows, and dark brown gardens. A narrow highway divided the town almost equally, leading south to Jerusalem and north to Damascus. Hafid nodded and smiled when Sergius pointed to the gathering of tiny figures still milling about the well.

To the west was Mount Carmel and beyond it they could see mist rising from the waters of the Mediterranean. Both men turned slowly, their mouths half open in awe, as they gazed at the wide plain of Esdraelon, Mount Tabor, the dark hills of Samaria, and the hazy mountains of Gilead. The Sea of Galilee glistened brightly to the east and far to the south the green valley of the Jordan seemed to change colors before their eyes. A light breeze noisily rustled the huge leaves of the ancient fig tree above them while far off, in the cloudless cobalt sky, a solitary eagle circled slowly, its wings fully extended but motionless.

Hafid was the first to break the strange silence of the hill but his words were spoken so slowly it was almost as if he were in a trance. "As many years as I have lived, I am positive that never before have I been at such an elevation with so much of the world at my feet. It is easy to understand why Jesus came here often. One's cares and problems all remain behind, down there," he said gesturing at the village, "and if there is a God I imagine it would be much easier to communicate with him from this height."

Sergius pointed far to the north toward the stately snow-covered crest of Mount Hermon, nearly two days' journey away and yet dominating the horizon. "God spoke to Jesus, once, on that high mountain."

"On Hermon? You have proof of that?"

"Three of his closest apostles were witnesses."

"And what did God say?"

"This is my beloved son; hear him."

"That is all?"

"That is everything," said Sergius, smiling.

"And you believe such a report from his three closest friends?"

"Enough so I have had a small home erected, on that mountain, as near to the place where the three reported hearing God's voice as it was possible to build. I keep the place well stocked with food, have a caretaker in residence through the entire year, and try to at least spend a fortnight there every summer. Many times I have been tempted to invite you to come share that special peace and tranquility with me but I knew you were in seclusion since your loss of Lisha and I did not want to disturb you. Now I would be most honored if you accepted my invitation to visit there. Bring Erasmus. Remain in that blessed retreat as long as you wish, please. Before we part I shall draw you a map so that you can easily locate my haven. It is less than a day's travel from your palace in Damascus."

"And has God also spoken to you, on that high place?"

"No, but I usually talk to him during my entire stay."

Hafid sighed and shook his head, raising the leather sack that held the robe of Jesus high above his head. "With your loving and trusting faith, Sergius, this robe should be in your possession, not mine."

"Oh, no," replied Sergius, raising his hands. "The mother of Jesus knew exactly what she was doing. The robe is in good hands. It is God's will."

Hafid rose and stood with hands on hips, staring at Mount Hermon. "If God were to speak to me, Sergius, what do you believe he might say about this new career on which I have perhaps foolishly embarked at my age?"

Sergius locked the fingers of his hands together, closed his eyes and bowed his head. After several moments he looked up at Hafid and when he spoke his voice had a deeper resonance than usual.

"I would never presume to speak for God, great salesman, but I imagine he would first congratulate you on your decision to remove thyself from the living dead. To devote the remainder of your days to helping others, through your sage advice and wise lessons on success, is most laudable, however . . ."

Hafid turned and looked down at his friend, waiting.

". . . however, if your speech last night was your usual presentation, as excellent as it was I believe it needs something more. For many who come to hear you, your reputation and great wealth are usually known and while they may be impressed by your presence and your delivery, there is a strong possibility that they are listening to your words with a closed mind . . . a mind that tells them they could never, never accomplish what you have accomplished. How do you open their minds? You can do that only by making them aware of your humble background, the struggles of your youth, and the handicaps you overcame in order to make your dreams come true."

"And how will I accomplish this?"

"By using the strongest of words to paint scenes in their minds they will never forget. Let them smell the camel dung you shoveled, let them see your tears of heartbreak, let them agonize over the failures you suffered as you were struggling to build a better life. Make them depart from your speech thinking, 'If Hafid was able to accomplish so much, with his lowly beginning, then why am I, with so much more, feeling sorry for my condition in life?' Since I doubt that you ever mention your early heartaches and struggles in your presentations, Hafid, you probably appear to those in your audience like some person of royalty who was born with a silver spoon in his mouth and has always enjoyed great wealth and success. How can a small merchant or farmer, who must struggle every day merely to put food on the table for his family, accept your message as a guide to change his life for the better when he does not realize that once you faced the same predicaments as he is facing and were victorious?"

"That is excellent advice, Sergius, and I shall heed it. Any more?"

Sergius opened his mouth but he lowered his eyes and remained silent.

"Please," encouraged Hafid. "We are as close as brothers. Speak your mind. Help me."

"Is there ample gold still in your treasury?"

"More than Erasmus and I shall ever need. Even now we are feeding and clothing multitudes, each day, in Damascus."

"As I expected. Hafid, there is a saying that is so old its source is lost in antiquity. 'Give a man a fish and you feed him for a day. Teach him how to fish and you feed him for a lifetime.' "

Hafid lowered himself to his knees, next to Sergius, and grasped his arm. "I am not certain that I understand how those words of wisdom relate to me."

"Like all other orators, you are charging admission for your speeches and so those who need your message the most do not hear it because they are too poor to attend. They are the same people you now feed and clothe. Change your procedure. Place your promoter, Galenus, on a weekly salary instead of his commission and send him out into the world with sufficient funds so that he can hire the largest possible forum for you in every city. Instruct him, also, to recruit and pay well as many townspeople as his experience dictates to spread the word as to where the greatest salesman in the world will speak, at what time, and announce that admission is free!"

"Free? There will be many who will attend only to be entertained or to pass the time of day with no thought of learning how to improve their lot in life."

"You are correct, without a doubt. Many men of great intellect insist that unless one has to pay or work hard for something, one never fully appreciates it. However, for all of those in your audiences on whom your words will probably be wasted, just imagine how satisfying it would be to you if you learned that there was at least one poor camel boy or street urchin in the crowd whose life might commence to take an upward path because of your words. I know how much you want to change the world for the better, my friend, but you must remember one thing . . . one simple truth."

"And what is that?"

"What you wish can only be accomplished by changing one person at a time."

Hafid leaned forward and embraced his beloved friend. "Thank you. If God had spoken, he could not have said it better."

VI

The Success Caravan, its name boldly
painted in red and gold lettering on all twelve of
its baggage wagons, in Latin, Greek, and Hebrew,
was encamped in an open meadow near the heart
of Rome. Inside the largest of many tents that
encircled the wagons, Hafid raised his wineglass
toward the goblets of Erasmus and Galenus. "To
our greatest victory," he announced proudly.

"It was, indeed, a night to remember," sighed
Erasmus.

Illuminated by more than two hundred oil
torches, installed around the raised stage and along
the aisles of Pompey's magnificent theater that
Augustus had later rebuilt, Hafid had delivered
his words of inspiration to a record throng of
more than eighteen thousand enthusiastic citizens
of Rome earlier in the evening. Clutching the frayed
red robe of Jesus, that he had worn on every
speech since his long-ago visit to Nazareth, Hafid

had joyfully acknowledged the rousing ovation that followed his closing remarks for almost an hour.

The great salesman sipped on his wine and said, "Galenus, I shall be forever grateful to you for convincing me to deliver these speeches in the evening rather than at midday as do all the others. Those we are most trying to reach, the less affluent laborers and small merchants of the city, could not possibly attend at any other time. Many have been heard to say that never before, in their entire lives, have they had the opportunity to hear a speaker."

"You were magnificent this evening, sire," replied Galenus, "and you seemed to handle the language like a native."

"Thank you. My only regret is that Sergius Paulus could not attend. Now that he has retired from office and returned here to Rome, I had looked forward to having him with us on this triumphal night; however, I pray that he recovers from his illness. I shall dispatch a message notifying him of our great success and he will be most pleased. Had it not been for his sage advice, more than fifteen years ago, we would not be here tonight and I probably would have joined my beloved Lisha, long ago, in our final resting place."

Galenus nodded. "I can still recall our early days with but a single wagon. Now our caravan has almost grown to the size of those employed by you during your busiest trade years. Besides our wagons we have sixteen camels and drivers plus eight armed guards with their mounts, two cooks, a dozen helpers, and more than forty horses to properly move us from city to city. Not to mention the fleet of ten vessels that it was necessary to charter in order to transport all of us, our equipment and our animals, from our previous engagement in Athens. We have straddled the world, sire, bringing your message, without charge, to the common people of Alexandria, Memphis, Jerusalem, Babylon, Baghdad, Nineveh, Aleppo, Edessa, Antioch, Ephesus, Smyrna, Sparta, Athens, hundreds of smaller cities, and now, the capital of the world, Rome. And when I hear how the people react to your words, I know you are touching thousands of lives."

Erasmus said, "Truly, it does not seem like fifteen years have passed since that chance meeting between the master and Sergius Paulus in Nazareth."

"I do not believe that was a chance meeting," said Hafid. "To me it was just another example of God playing chess with me as he has done so often in my life. I am convinced that occasionally he intercedes in all of our lives and causes things to happen. Then he waits to see how we deal with his move. Some react in a manner that will enhance their future. Others may fight back with anger and despair. And then there are those who act not at all. They are the living dead and we have many of those among us, spending their days whining and complaining and never making any attempt to change their lives for the better.

That is why I devote so much of my talk to teaching the poor and the downtrodden, the weak and the handicapped, how to deal with any move that confronts them, always reminding these struggling members of humanity that while God does challenge us, he wants us all to be victorious. I'm trying to teach them how to win and nothing is more satisfying to me than to return to a city, years later, and listen to the success stories that began when someone heard my words and took them to heart."

"And now," Erasmus said hesitantly, "we are strangers on Roman soil where the emperor actually believes he is a god who controls the lives of all his subjects from his palace of gold. We can be certain there were spies in our audience, tonight, checking as to whether there was any danger of Hafid's words inciting the masses just as the followers of Jesus were accused of doing with their songs of a kingdom to come and a kingdom within. Nero even blamed them for starting the great conflagration last year and those who were not arrested and executed in the arena are still hiding in the catacombs beneath the city. Their faith, I'm afraid, has had a terrible price."

"I wonder," said Hafid smiling, "how Nero would react if he knew that the robe I wear, when I speak, belonged to Jesus."

"Please, sire," Erasmus pleaded softly, "let that be our little secret."

The sentry standing guard outside the big

tent leaned through the opening and announced that Hafid had a visitor.

"Bid him enter!" shouted Hafid as he refilled the wineglasses.

Their guest wore a dark blue tunic, tied at the waist with cord and cut low to the ground. His long brown hair was streaked with grey and his tanned face was etched with deep wrinkles. When he spoke his voice was friendly and strong.

"Grace be to you, and peace. My name is Luke and I come with a message for the greatest salesman in the world from his old friend, Paul of Tarsus."

Hafid leaped to his feet. "Paul is here, here in Rome?"

"He is a prisoner in the Praetorium, awaiting trial."

"That cannot be," protested Hafid. "His most recent letter contained the good news that he had finally been freed for lack of evidence after suffering in chains for four years in Caesarea and Rome."

"He has been arrested again and this time they claim to have witnesses who will testify that Paul was heard proclaiming that Jesus is king. Under Roman law, to recognize any other authority but Caesar is a crime punishable by death."

"Is there anything I can do?" asked Hafid. "Tell me, please."

"Since his arrest, this time, Paul seems to have lost his will to live. Most of his friends and followers have deserted him and he just sits in his cell, saying little and eating only scraps of dried bread. I had feared for his health until this morning when I informed him that banners were flying along the Appian Way proclaiming your appearance at Pompey's Theater. Only after he heard your name, sire, did he commence acting like the man I have served for so long. He sends you his love, illustrious salesman, welcomes you to Rome, and begs that you visit him at the prison. Since we have no information as to when Paul will be tried, I hope that you will see him soon."

"Any time," said Hafid without hesitation. "When can you take me?"

"There are no days and nights in the dark cells of that hated place. I am trusted by the officers there. We can go even now if you are not too weary."

Erasmus was frowning at Luke. "The master forgets, very often, that he is nearly seventy-five years old. His performance, this night, has drained much of his energy and he should be in bed."

"No," said Hafid. "I am never too tired if that man of God is calling me. Take me now, Luke."

As they were leaving, Hafid stopped at his open clothes closet near the center pole. He reached in and removed the robe of Jesus, tossing it over his shoulders as he stepped outside. "Perhaps seeing this special and blessed garment, again," he explained to Luke, "will lift Paul's spirits as it always does mine."

The grey and somber prison on Capitaline Hill, near the palace of Nero, served to house only prisoners who had committed grave crimes against the state. It was guarded by a special cohort of veteran legionaries under the command of the prefect of the entire Praetorian cohort. No one had ever escaped from its cells. Luke was recognized by the officer inside the door on the main floor and after a brief wait he and Hafid were led down a steep flight of stone steps. The slate floor was moist and there was a damp chill in the air as the two followed the tall guard along a rat-infested corridor until he stopped before a cell and turned his key in the door. "It will be necessary to lock you both in with the prisoner," he said, "but do not be concerned. When you are prepared to depart, merely call out and I shall come."

He held the door ajar until both men had entered the dimly lit cell. Then he allowed it to swing closed and the clashing of iron bars reverberated throughout the lower floor.

"Luke," a hoarse voice called from the darkest corner. "Luke, is that you?"

"Yes, Paul, and see . . . I have brought a friend!"

The great salesman's eyes were gradually becoming accustomed to the shadowy interior of the small cell and yet he felt hands on his arms before he saw the face of Paul. "Hafid," the little man sobbed, "is it you? Is it truly you? My great friend and benefactor! He who saved my life by presenting me with the scrolls of success, long ago, that enabled me to sell the message of my lord to the world! So many times I have wanted to visit with you, in Damascus, but always my friends warned me that you were in seclusion and saw no one. Yet, never in my letters could I convey the great debt I owe to you. I am so sorry to see you under these conditions but I give thanks to God that you came. The years, I am pleased to note, have been kind to thee."

Now Hafid could see Paul's emaciated face which was dominated by two large eyes beneath heavy eyebrows and a wide, scarred forehead. His hair, matted and unkempt, fell loosely over his emaciated cheeks and his tattered loincloth offered scant protection from the cold. Paul clung to Hafid as would a frightened child to his parent. Finally Luke pointed to a small unpainted table. "Come," he said, "let us sit and talk."

Paul needed no further encouragement. In response to only a few questions from his two visitors, he spoke at length of his long-ago vision on the road to Damascus and how his life had changed forever. He recalled his visit to Hafid and the gift of the scrolls, his many journeys to the great cities of the world, his previous imprisonments, his nearly fatal shipwreck on the isle of Malta, and his constant battle to spread his message to the people beyond the borders of Palestine with only a few helpers and little funds. His voice grew in strength as he continued to talk but finally it broke and he grinned shyly, suddenly realizing how much he had dominated the conversation. "Forgive me, dear friends. I have been alone here too long. Any good preacher, given an audience of any size, will go on forever anyway, is that not true, great salesman?"

Hafid smiled and shrugged his shoulders. "I would not know since I am not a preacher."

"Oh ho!" exclaimed Paul, turning to Luke. "Listen to this man! Hafid, whether you realize it or not, you and I are in the same business. We are both fighting to rescue people, men and women, from hell. The hell you are trying to save them from is here . . . and now. The hell I want to protect them from is tomorrow . . . and forever. We are both struggling to convince those who will listen that living in heaven here, and heaven for eternity, requires the same qualities of loving, caring, charity, and hard work. I have never heard you deliver your famous speech, sire, but my friends have informed me that the principles of good living that you proclaim could just as easily have been delivered by Moses or Solomon or Isaiah . . . or Jesus. Your words, I am told, seem to spring from your soul with great power and they influence the minds and hearts of all who hear you. That is a great gift, Hafid. I only regret that you are not in our camp." He stroked the red robe on Hafid's back. "But then," he smiled, "perhaps you are without even realizing it."

Hafid's legs were becoming numb from the cold. He rose and commenced pacing back and forth in the small cell. "The scrolls that I passed on to you, so very long ago, what has become of them?"

"All my possessions were lost in that shipwreck last year. I had managed to keep the scrolls by my side for almost thirty years, even in prisons; however, the ocean finally claimed them. All ten, however, are as much a part of me as my eyes or my hands. I can recall and recite each scroll, word for word, and I have lost count of the number of times they saved my life by guiding me on the correct path each day."

Hafid winced and closed his eyes, swaying back on his heels as if he had been struck. He turned his back on his two friends and rested his head wearily against the iron bars. Finally he said softly, "Those precious leather rolls were so filled with power and life that somehow I have always taken it for granted that they were imperishable. Still, if they survived until last year, they were already more than a hundred years old by my calculation. Tell me, Paul, did you share the wisdom of the scrolls at every opportunity, as I had instructed, so that others might be resurrected from a living death and enjoy a new life filled with happiness, achievement, and love?"

"Everywhere that my travels took me, great salesman, just as I promised you. Whenever I managed to convert another, I would also teach the principles of the scrolls so that he or she might be better equipped to carry forth and sell the truth to others. During the past ten years, especially, there have been hundreds, perhaps thousands of copies, both papyrus and leather, made and circulated throughout the world . . . from Jerusalem to Rome."

Hafid reached out and stroked Paul's matted hair with both his hands. "You have traveled far beyond the extra mile, great messenger. Instead of this vile home for rodents, mankind should be paying you homage in a palace of gold and silver. My heart is heavy and I feel so helpless. What is ahead for thee?"

Paul crossed his arms over his thin bare chest. His voice was calm. "The time of my final departure, I fear, is at hand. I am ready. I have fought the good fight and I believe I have finished my course. Luke, here, has been trusted ally and companion for many years and I have finally convinced him to transcribe what he has learned from me onto parchment. He has almost completed that long task after many months and now I have some hope that my message might outlive me. And you, Hafid, have your principles of success, your golden thoughts, been written down so that generations to come may continue to benefit from the essence of your great speech?"

"No, not as yet."

"You must do it . . . and soon. We know not the hour or the day when God will beckon us to join him and it would be a great loss to the world for your secrets of achievement and happiness to be entombed with thee. Promise me you will attend to that and soon."

Hafid forced a smile and patted Paul's sunken cheek. "I promise."

Paul nodded. "And when you do, please consider using the same form as those original ten scrolls which had such a great influence on both our lives. I doubt that there has ever been a more powerful technique for training anyone to succeed than the system utilized in those scrolls. Combining that method, once more, with your great knowledge will produce results that are certain to work miracles in many lives. And do not wait, I beg of thee!"

The jailor now stood outside the prison door. It was time to depart. Paul first embraced Luke and then stepped close to Hafid who wrapped his arms around the apostle's frail and half-naked body.

"May the Lord preserve you unto his heavenly kingdom," Paul said, inhaling deeply. "Great salesman, I thank God whom I serve, for having made you a part of my life."

Paul stepped back as the cell door swung open and Luke walked out into the hall. The jailor waited impatiently when Hafid paused in the doorway and turned, quickly removing his red robe which he then wrapped around the thin shoulders of the shivering apostle.

"Stay warm, dear friend," said Hafid. "I love you."

"I love you, too. Forever!"

VII

$\mathcal{E}$rasmus fell back as if he had been struck. "I am not certain that my old ears heard correctly, master."

Hafid's voice signaled his weariness. "I said that it was very cold in that terrible dungeon, last night, and Paul had little clothing so I gave him my robe."

"But you have delivered at least eight hundred speeches, through all these years, with that old and worn garment of Jesus' about your person. Many times I have heard you say that to feel it on your shoulders lifted your spirits and filled you with confidence. How will you function without it, should it not be returned in time for your next speech?"

Hafid closed his eyes and said, "I have little hope of ever seeing the robe again since I fear that Paul's days are numbered. Even he, who has spent his life challenging great odds, has admitted that the end is near. Let the robe comfort our brave little friend in his final days."

"But can you perform without it?" asked Galenus anxiously.

"It will not be necessary. I know that both you and Erasmus have made plans to continue north to Pisa and Genoa and possibly into Gaul and I beg your forgiveness for this sudden decision; however, my speaking career has ended. Last night was my final act from the platform."

Erasmus moved closer and stared directly into Hafid's eyes. "Are you ill, master? Shall I secure a physician?"

"Have you already forgotten that last night I was in the company of Luke, a wise and experienced man of medicine? No, Erasmus, I am in good health. However, I was unable to sleep, last night, after returning from that prison. The parting words of Paul weighed heavily on my mind and my heart and I have decided to follow his wise advice while I still have my good health."

"I do not understand, sire."

"We are dining with Sergius Paulus and wife at his villa this evening, are we not?"

"Yes. The invitation to all three of us was delivered after you and Luke had departed for the prison, last night."

"Then I beg of you, please be patient for a few more hours and I shall make my plans for the future known to all, at the dinner."

The retired governor's villa, nestled in the foothills west of the Tiber, was not as large as the

palace on Cyprus but it contained a spacious dining room that had already become a favorite of
Rome's aristocracy. Its walls were inlaid with
mother-of-pearl while the silk-covered ceiling contained hundreds of openings into which fresh cut
flowers were inserted each day. Marble statues of
every Caesar stood guard around the room and in
its center was an immense circular bronze table
inlaid with ivory and gold.

There were only four guests at dinner and
they were clustered at one end of the huge table,
two on each side of Sergius Paulus and his wife of
forty years, Cornelia, who smiled frequently but
said little during the meal. Joining Hafid, Erasmus, and Galenus was the celebrated poet, essay-
ist, attorney, and orator, Seneca, who once had
been Nero's tutor, consul, and virtual prime minister for many years before retiring to his nearby
estate only four years ago. He had partaken of
little food, during the many servings, and when
Hafid sympathized with his difficulty in breathing
he replied that he had suffered from asthma for
many years and now all he was doing was practicing how to die by taking last gulps every time he
inhaled.

Hafid said, "I have read many of your works,
sir, and I am honored to be in the same room with
you."

Seneca's pale cheeks turned crimson. "That is
very kind, mighty salesman, however it is I who
am most grateful to the governor for giving me
this opportunity to meet you. I have admired your

accomplishments for decades, first in trade and now in oratory, and never dreamed that our paths would cross. To have reached the very pinnacle of success in two unrelated professions as you have done is a rare feat and I salute you. Last night I attended your inspiring speech and listened with great interest to your message. I agree with your philosophy regarding the best way to deal with this life."

"Thank you."

Seneca raised his hand and nodded. "Most of all I applaud your great honesty when you commenced your talk by admitting how much you still had to learn about our world because you were only a small fragment in this infinite universe. Many so-called wise men, bloated with a false sense of worth, never admit that all of us are only fleeting moments in eternity. Coming from a man of your stature, that was an unusual confession."

"I was only being honest," replied Hafid. "Tell me, is it true that you are no longer involved in the affairs of Rome in any way?"

Seneca chuckled. "I struggled for many years to convert a monster into a human being and obviously failed. A few years ago I transferred most of my wealth to Nero in exchange for his permission to leave government. Now I spend my days in quiet contemplation as well as putting as many of my thoughts and conclusions on parchment as I can before our mad emperor decides that even I, in my senile years, am a threat to him and should die."

Hafid raised his wineglass. "We still have much to learn from you. May you live another fifty years."

"And how is it with you, Hafid?" Seneca asked after he had sipped his wine. "Is it not true that you owe much of your great success to wisdom you learned from ten special scrolls that were a gift when you were a youth? Are you making arrangements to pass on your legacy by transcribing your wise principles of success and living onto scrolls for tomorrow's children? Although Nero's sword does not hang over your head, as it does mine, you must realize that you, too, are approaching that fateful day when you will take your final gasp of precious air."

Before Hafid could reply, Luke burst into the room followed by two servants apologizing for the intrusion to their master. The old physician's breath came in noisy gasps as if he had been running a long distance. Heavy perspiration covered his brow.

"Please forgive me for besmirching this happy and peaceful gathering," he said between breaths, "but I regret being the bearer of sad news that I knew you would all want to know as swiftly as possible."

"Dear Luke, you look exhausted," said a concerned Sergius. "Here, take this seat and gather thy thoughts. Perhaps a drink of wine?"

"No," Luke protested, fighting back tears. "Please let me stand! I have just come from the prison. There I was informed that Paul was tried this morning and found guilty of treason against Rome."

Luke lowered his head. "He was comdemned to death and immediately led out to a small plot of public land near the Ostian Way and beheaded. There were," he sobbed, "no witnesses or friends present. The authorities presented me with his remains, in a sack, when I arrived there tonight and, although the sun had set, I buried our friend in the garden of a follower who lives near the Praetorium."

"And what of the red robe he was wearing?" asked Erasmus, immediately regretting his words when he saw Hafid angrily glaring at him.

Luke wiped away his tears. "Only his . . . his remains were in the sack. In my grief I never thought to ask about the robe. I fear that it is lost."

Hafid stood and placed his arm gently on Luke's shoulder. His words were for everyone. "Let us pray for him often, of course, but let us never shed any tears of grief over our beloved Paul. Where he is, this evening, he would change places with none of us."

"I am amazed, constantly amazed," Seneca said, "at the lack of fear with which those who follow Jesus have faced death, horrible deaths, in the arena, on the chopping block, and even hanging from a cross. For more years than I want to count, I have been hearing rumors that the body of Jesus was removed from the tomb by his closest disciples who then hid the body and claimed that he was God because he had risen from the dead. However, last week, here in Rome, the man reputed to be closest to Jesus, Peter, was told his life would be spared if only he would admit to authorities that Jesus had not risen from the dead. Peter was crucified, I have been told, upside down at his request, so as not to die in the same manner that Jesus did. Now, if Peter knew that the body of Jesus had been removed from the tomb—and he, of all people, would have had knowledge of that deed if it had been committed—why was he still willing to die for a lie? And now the brilliant Paul has also given his life. I don't know! I don't know! There is so much about all of this that I do not comprehend. I do know, however, that if I were a younger man, with my life still ahead of me, I would seek to know more of this man called Jesus and what he taught."

"One is never too old, Seneca," Sergius said. "We would welcome you with open arms."

"We? Has the distinguished Roman governor of Cyprus, for so many years, turned his back on the gods of Rome? Are you one of them?"

"I am."

Seneca shook his head in disbelief and turned to Hafid. "And what of thee, greatest salesman of them all. To whom do you bow?"

"Once I bowed to no man, not even Caesar. But one day, many years ago, Sergius Paulus and I climbed the highest hill overlooking the tiny village of Nazareth, after we had visited the mother of Jesus. Sitting up there, so close to heaven, I suddenly realized that my lifelong search for a faith that would always guide and sustain me had ended. I knew, without any doubt, that the sack I had received from Mary contained far more than the seamless red robe of another poor preacher. I was positive that I had, in my possession, the cloak that had for so long protected the body of the son of God."

Sergius Paulus leaned forward and kissed the great salesman's cheek. No words were spoken.

Later, as Hafid, Luke, and Erasmus were returning to the caravan, Erasmus leaned close to his master and asked, "What of our future, sire? Whither shall we go next?"

"We shall return to Damascus," Hafid replied, "as soon as all arrangements can be made and there we shall disband the caravan. I plan to retire to my library and take as much time as God allows to transcribe my ten most important principles for a good life onto scrolls similar in form to those that were given to me when I was a mere camel boy."

"And then . . . ?" asked Erasmus.

"And then I shall be prepared to assist you in supervising an organization of swift messengers who can deliver copies of my scrolls to the four corners of the world. We can reach millions in that manner, instead of the thousands who came to hear me speak."

"I would be honored to assist thee in thy great task," said Luke. "My handwriting is excellent and I would be willing to transcribe the words you speak onto parchment."

"Physician, you have a more important mission. Do as Paul asked of you. Write down all you know of his struggles and travels and also write down all you have learned of the life of Jesus, including the story of his birth in that stable in Bethlehem that I related to thee when we walked back to my wagons last night."

"Hafid," Sergius cried out. "I have just been blessed with a most powerful idea. Remember my telling you, when we were together in Nazareth long ago, of the home I had built on Mount Hermon, a retreat that is very close to where God spoke to Jesus?"

"I do and I have regretted, many times, that I never accepted your generous invitation to visit there."

"It is not too late. Hear me through. I am too old, now, to travel to Mount Hermon any longer, and so I shall soon be transferring ownership of that special place to my caretaker, Stephanas, who has served me loyally at that location all these years. To be close to where God spoke would make a perfect setting for you while you are concentrating and creating the ten scrolls."

"The road from the port of Sidon to Damascus passes very close to the mountain," said Galenus encouragingly.

"And what of Stephanas?" asked Hafid.

"Stephanas, on my written instructions which you will deliver, can easily return to his family, in nearby Caesarea Philippi, and leave you in complete seclusion until you finish your project. What an ideal place to do your very best work! Only the wind will disturb your concentration unless, of course, God decides to talk with you. Then, when you are finished, you can return to your palace in Damascus, only half a day's journey away, and Erasmus can supervise the circulation of your inspiring words."

Hafid looked at Erasmus who remained silent. This was a decision he would have to make on his own.

Sergius Paulus continued. "Now is your final opportunity, Hafid. Next year, Stephanas and all his family will probably reside in that house. Go, I beg of you!"

VIII

$\mathcal{B}$efore the caravan departed from Rome,
Hafid, with Luke as his guide, visited scores of
shops in the nearby book district called Argiletum.
After hours of shopping he had finally purchased
several bottles of the finest black ink imported
from Egypt, a box of metal pens and goose quills,
and a dozen unused parchment scrolls prepared
from the dried skins of goat.

It was already mid-afternoon when the two
finally decided to return to the caravan and they
had proceeded no more than fifty paces when
Hafid suddenly halted and pointed toward a dark-
stained, bruised cedar chest that was lying on its
side near an outside bookstall. "Is that old chest
empty?" he cried out excitedly to the dozing merchant who was leaning on a nearby table.

"It is not only empty, sir, it is also for sale."

Hafid stepped closer. His voice was trembling.
"Will you kindly open it for me?"

The tradesman lifted the trunk onto the table and threw back the latch. Then he raised its wooden top and allowed it to fall back, exposing the dusty interior.

Hafid turned to a puzzled Luke. "Hand me some of the scrolls that we purchased."

Luke reached into the leather sack he had been carrying and removed three scrolls. Hafid placed them gently inside the trunk. "Now, give me seven more, please."

The seven filled the trunk to the top. Hafid closed the cover gently and turned to the merchant. "How much?"

"Only a hundred denarii, sir."

Hafid reached inside his cloak for his money bag but Luke stopped him. "Sir," he protested, "that price is ten times too high for this old box! See how rusty the hinges are and the strappings are so worn. Come, I know a fine shop near here where you will find a variety of trunks more suitable to your needs and at a much fairer price."

"Luke, I appreciate your concern but this is the chest I want. I cannot believe my old eyes but it looks exactly like the trunk that contained the ten scrolls I received when I was a camel boy more than sixty years ago."

Luke smiled patiently. "It appears old enough and worn enough to be that very same chest."

Hafid paid the merchant and said, "It is not just a coincidence that I discovered this chest at this time in my life. Here is God playing chess with me again and this is a good sign. Now I shall have the perfect container for my scrolls after they have been written!"

Two weeks passed before the Success Caravan finally docked at the port of Sidon and a day later they had arrived at the crossroads that led east to Damascus and south to Mount Hermon.

Hafid climbed down from the large carriage that had served him and the others for so many years on his speaking tours. Behind was a smaller carriage filled with cases of food, clothing, and his writing supplies. The driver of the smaller wagon approached his leader and said, "Everything is in order, sire," as he handed his whip to Hafid. By now, Erasmus and Galenus had joined their master. Hafid turned to his old bookkeeper and said, "I shall return to our home as soon as I have completed work on the scrolls, perhaps in a fortnight or so."

Erasmus was unable to hide his concern. "Master, will ye kindly reconsider thy decision and allow me to accompany thee? It has been many, many years since we have been apart."

"Rid thyself of fear, Erasmus. I must do this alone so that my concentration is unbroken. I shall survive. The weather is warm and I have ample food for several weeks. Soon we shall be reunited. Do you still have your copy of the maps that Sergius Paulus gave both of us, the directions to the house on Hermon?"

Erasmus patted his robe. "It is here, sire."

Hafid nodded as he drew his faithful friend to his bosom. "If you should become lonely after a month or so and I have not returned, you are welcome to pay me a visit. For now, return to our home in Damascus and take Galenus with you for company, as we agreed. He will also be of great help in your disbanding of the caravan. I bid thee farewell, for the moment. Tonight, I shall sleep alone at the place where God once spoke."

The road from the base of Mount Hermon rose so gradually that it was difficult for Hafid to realize that he was now climbing the majestic mountain that, viewed from a distance, seemed to touch heaven. He did not hurry his two stallions since he was savoring the fragrant slopes with their ilex, hawthorn, and almond trees while hyacinths, cyclamen, and buttercups flourished along the roadside. After more than an hour, he passed a giant column of rough white stone, rising more than fifty cubits from mounds of small boulders, and he knew, according to his map, that he was now only two miles from his destination.

To his left, as he rode, the world seemed to be spread out for his enjoyment. Far off, light sparkled from the Sea of Galilee and the great salesman strained to catch a glimpse of his beloved Damascus, to the east, but a heavy mist hung over the desert in that direction. To his right, high above, he could see the mountaintop and realized that the snow, which at a distance seemed to be an unbroken mantle of glistening white, was actually only in the hollows and clefts.

The map that Sergius Paulus had drawn indicated that the road would eventually wind through

a grove of wild mountain junipers which concealed, from passing travelers, the old governor's
home. As soon as the wagon was beneath the
green boughs, Hafid quickly brought it to a stop.
Directly ahead, with the lower branches of several
trees resting on its roof, was Hafid's destination.

A wide-shouldered man, dressed in animal
skins, was standing by the front door of the small
house, watching curiously as Hafid dismounted
from his wagon. He waited, uncertainly, until the
great salesman raised his hand in greeting before
calling out, "Are ye lost, stranger?"

"I think not. You are Stephanas?"

"I am."

"Your friend and employer, Sergius Paulus,
sends you his greetings. Also, a letter for you
with instructions."

Stephanas accepted the small parchment roll,
broke the seal, and hastily read the words. Then
he bowed respectfully toward Hafid and said, "Welcome, sire. Let me bring in your baggage and help
you to become settled in this special place."

Hafid grasped the younger man's right hand
and placed two gold coins in his calloused palm.
"I regret, very much, driving you from your home;
however, it will not be for long and Sergius has
somewhat eased my concern by informing me that
you have family nearby."

Stephanas nodded, staring in disbelief at his
newly acquired wealth. "I have felt remorse, many
times, for not yet visiting my mother and father
this summer. Now will be a good time."

The house contained only four rooms but it was decorated and furnished with the same good taste that Sergius had used in both his palace and his villa. Most pleasing to Hafid was the large writing table on which he placed his pens, ink, and scrolls. The old chest he had purchased in Rome was pushed under the table. After Stephanas had unloaded the food and other supplies from the wagon, he carried in several logs for the huge, stone fireplace.

"Before I depart, sire, do you have any questions? Is there anything else I can show you?"

Hafid had been staring out the open door at the shadowy grove of trees to the rear of the house. "Yes," he replied softly, "can you lead me to the place where God was heard to speak?"

"Come," said Stephanas, and he guided the older man along a path that was overrun with daisies. Finally he stopped and leaned against a tree. "Peter returned to this place, accompanied by Sergius, only a few years ago and he said it all happened here. See, I have arranged a circle of boulders to mark the area. Apparently Peter and James and John had accompanied Jesus from Caesarea Philippi and the three were so weary that they fell asleep on this ground, soon after they arrived. Peter said that they awoke to a light that almost blinded them, shining from where Jesus had knelt and was still praying. Then a bright cloud descended on them and in the stillness they heard a voice saying, 'This is my beloved son; hear him.' "

"What happened then?" asked Hafid.

"It was over, Peter said, within minutes. The cloud soon faded away and only the stars above were witness."

Hafid stepped over the large boulders and walked slowly on the uneven ground until he was close to the middle of the circle. Despite the chill, he felt a sudden warm breeze across his face and the pounding of his heart. The voice of Stephanas startled him. "If there is nothing else I can do for you, I shall depart so that I can be off the mountain before the sun sets."

Hafid watched the retreating figure of Stephanas until it vanished in the dusk. Then he knelt near the largest boulder and placed his folded hands on its rough surface. Once again he felt that mysterious warm breeze and he knew that part of his daily routine, so long as he remained on the mountain, would be to kneel at this same stone, each morning, to pray for help in completing his scrolls.

He slept little that night, staring up at the darkness and planning what he would write. "This," he said aloud, "is the greatest challenge of my life. I have been honored for my trade empire and for my oratory but to be able to fashion words on parchment with the power to change the future of those who read them is the supreme accomplishment and a miracle unto itself. I know that I cannot accomplish this almost impossible undertaking alone. Help me, God, I beg of you."

When morning came, Hafid ate a light breakfast and walked outside. He inhaled deeply, several times, and then approached the circle of boulders where he knelt and once again prayed for help. Then he returned to the house, assumed a comfortable position in the leather-covered chair at the writing table, opened a clean scroll, dipped his quill into the dark ink, and began to write. . . .

Twice each day, in the morning and in the evening before I retire, I will read the words on this scroll. The evening reading must be aloud. I will continue in this manner for seven days, including the Sabbath, before proceeding to the next numbered scroll. Thus, in ten weeks, I will have completed my foundation for building a new and better life.

I understand that no provision has been made should I neglect one or more daily readings. As in life itself, I realize that the amount of success I am able to achieve through this wisdom will be in direct proportion to the effort expended in acquiring it. . . . . . .

IX

THE FIRST
VOW OF SUCCESS

I was born to succeed, not to fail.

I was born to triumph, not to bow my head in defeat.

I was born to toast victories, not to whimper and whine.

What happened to me? When did my dreams all fade into a grey mediocrity where average people applaud each other as excellent?

No person is ever so much deceived by another, as by himself. The coward is convinced that he is only being cautious and the miser always thinks he is practicing frugality. Nothing is so easy as to deceive one's self since what we wish is always easy to believe. No one, in my life, has deceived me as much as I have.

Why do I always try to cover my small

accomplishments under blankets of words that make light of my work or excuses for my lack of ability? Worst of all, I have come to believe my excuses so that I willingly sell my days for pennies while consoling myself with thoughts that things could always be worse.

No more!

It is time to study the reflection in my looking glass until I recognize that the most harmful enemy I have . . . is me. At last, in this magic moment with my first scroll, the veil of self-deceit is beginning to lift from my eyes.

Now I know that there are three classes of people in the world. The first learn from their own experience—these are wise. The second learn from the experience of others— these are happy. The third learn neither from their own experience nor from the experience of others—these are fools.

I am not a fool. Henceforth I will stand on my own feet and my terrible crutches of self-pity and self-contempt have been cast aside forever.

Never again will I pity or belittle myself.

How foolish I was when I stood in despair, by the side of the road, and envied the successful and the wealthy as they paraded by. Are they blessed with unique skills, rare intelligence, heroic courage, enduring ambition, and other outstanding qualities that I possess not? Have they been allotted more hours, each day, in which to perform their mighty tasks? Do they have hearts full of compassion and souls overflowing with love that are different from mine? No! God plays no favorites. We were all fashioned from the same clay.

Now I also know that the sadness and setbacks of my life are not unique to me. Even the wisest and most successful of our world suffer chapters of heartbreak and failure but they, unlike me, have learned that there is no peace without trouble, no rest without strain, no laughter without sorrow, no victory without struggle and that is the price we all pay for living. There was a time when I paid the price willingly and easily but constant disappointments and defeats first eroded my confidence and then my courage even as drops of water will, in time, destroy the strongest granite. All that is now behind me. No longer am I one of the living dead, remaining always in the shadows of others and hiding behind my sorry apologies and alibis while the years waste away.

Never again will I pity or belittle myself.

Now I know that patience and time can do more than even strength and passion. The years of frustration are ready to be harvested.

All that I have managed to accomplish, and all that I hope to accomplish, has been and will be by that plodding, patient, persevering process which builds the ant heap, particle by particle, thought by thought, step by step.

Success, when it comes overnight, often departs with the dawn. I am prepared, now, for a lifetime of happiness because I have finally recognized a powerful secret hidden in the years that treated me so harshly. Failure is, in a sense, the highway to success, inasmuch as every discovery we make of what is false leads us to seek earnestly after what is true and every fresh experience points out some form of error which we shall afterward carefully avoid. The path I walked, often dampened by my tears, has not been a wasted journey.

Never again will I pity or belittle myself.

Thank you, God, for playing your game with me, today, and placing in my hands these precious scrolls. I was at the lowest ebb of my life but I should have known it is at that moment that the tide always turns.

No longer will I look mournfully to the past. It will never return. Instead, with these scrolls, I will shape the present because it is mine and I will go forth to meet the mysterious future without fear, without doubt, without despair.

I was formed in the image of God. There is nothing I cannot achieve if I try.

Never again will I pity or belittle myself.

X

THE SECOND
VOW OF SUCCESS

*A*lready I am a different and better person.

Only a few days have passed since I commenced a new existence with the help of these scrolls but now there is a strange and powerful stirring in my heart, a feeling of new hope that had all but disappeared with the passing years.

At last I have been rescued from my cot of despair and I give thanks. With the words from the first vow of success still fresh on my lips, I have already multiplied in value in my eyes and this new assessment of me, I am certain, will eventually be adopted by the outside world. Now I know a great truth. The only valid price tag is the one we attach to ourselves. If we price ourselves too low, the world will agree. But if we price ourselves with the very best, the world also willingly accepts that valuation.

Thank you, God, for placing these precious scrolls in my hands. This is the turning point in my life and I must not, I will not, walk away from this challenge as I have so many in the past. Now I know that in everyone's pilgrimage through this life there are holy places were one is made to feel kinship with the divine; where the heavens seem to bend low over our heads and the angels come and minister to us. These are the places of sacrifice, the meeting grounds of mortal and immortal, the tents of the trial where are waged the great battles of one's life. My defeats of the past are already almost forgotten. Even the pain and the heartbreak. And happy will I be, in years to come, if I am able to look back on this special time and know that here, at last, I tasted victory.

But first I must learn and put into practice the second vow of success:

Never again will I greet the dawn without a map.

In the past, to have any goals, either large or small, seemed no more than an exercise in foolishness since I had so little faith in my abilities. Why have small and insignificant goals, I asked myself, merely to satisfy my lowly talents? What difference did it make in the scheme of things? And so, each day I would stumble out into the world, rudderless and chartless, hoping to survive until sunset, falsely assuring myself that I was only waiting for the proper moment or for my luck to change yet never believing for a single moment that anything in my future would be any different from my past.

To drift from day to day is easy. No skill is required, nor effort nor pain. On the other hand to set goals for a day or a week or a month, and to attain those objectives, is never easy. Tomorrow I will begin, I told myself day after day. I didn't know, then, that tomorrow is only found in the calendars of fools. Blind to my foolish faults, I was wasting my life in deliberation for I know not what and I would have procrastinated until it was too late had it not been for these scrolls. There is an immeasurable distance between late and too late.

Never again will I greet the dawn without a map.

I have been living in fool's alley. To be always intending to make a new and better life but never to find time to set about it is as if I should put off eating and drinking and sleeping from one day to the next until I am dead. For too many years I was convinced,

like so many others, that the only worthwhile
goals were princely goals with rich rewards
in gold and fame and power. How wrong I
have been. Now I know that the wise man
never makes goals of immense proportions.
Those plans that are giant in size he calls
dreams and cradles them close to his heart
where others may not see and mock. Then he
greets each morning with goals for the day
only and he makes certain that all he has
planned is completed before he sleeps. Soon
the accomplishments of each day are gathered,
one atop another, like the ant piles his grains
of sand, and eventually a castle is erected
large enough to house any dream. In truth,
this is not difficult to accomplish once I have
learned to harness my impatience and deal
with life a day at a time. I can do it. I will do it.

*Never again will I greet the dawn without a
map.*

The victory of success is half won when
one gains the habit of setting goals and achieving them. Even the most tedious chore will
become endurable as I parade through each
day convinced that every task, no matter how
menial or boring, brings me steps closer to
fulfilling my dreams. What a pleasant way to
get on with my life for if the morning presented me with no new joys, as I fulfill my
goals for the day, or if the evening delivered

me no new pleasures for completing my goals, it would not be worthwhile even to dress and undress. Life, I am now convinced, can be as joyful as children at play when one awakes with anticipation that a path clearly marked is waiting.

I know, now, where I am.

I know, also, where I want my goals to take me.

To get from here to there, I need not know all the twists and turns of my voyage at this moment. What is most important is that I have embraced the first scroll and the second and now I will never look back on that dismal past when days had no beginning or end and I was lost in a desert of futility with nothing ahead but death and failure.

Tomorrow I will have goals! And the next day! And the next!

Never again will I greet the dawn without a map.

Once I did bargain with life for a penny and life would pay no more, but my years of working for slave's wages have ended. Now I know that whatever wage I had asked of life, life would have willingly paid.

The sun is not shining on me so that I may reflect with sadness on yesterday. The past is buried and I almost allowed myself to be buried with it. No more tears. Let the sun's rays shine on tomorrow's promises . . . and me.

Never again will I greet the dawn without a map.

XI

THE THIRD
VOW OF SUCCESS

I am awake.

I am filled with joyful anticipation.

I feel unfamiliar rumblings in my heart as I welcome each new day, now, with joy and confidence instead of self-pity and fear.

He who suffers, remembers. I will never repeat the failures and futile mistakes of the past now that I have these scrolls to guide me.

Each day, I will venture out into the world accompanied by three powerful new allies: confidence, pride, and enthusiasm. I am confident I can deal with any challenge, pride demands that I perform to the best of my ability, and all this will be accomplished because I have rediscovered a special power that has been missing from my life since childhood, the power of enthusiasm.

Every memorable act in the history of the world is a triumph of enthusiasm. Nothing great was ever achieved without it because it gives any challenge or any occupation, no matter how frightening or difficult, a new meaning. Without enthusiasm I am doomed to a life of mediocrity but with it I can accomplish miracles.

There is a new meaning to my existence. Failure is no longer my constant companion. The nothingness, isolation, powerlessness, sadness, vexation, and despair of the past have vanished since that day, not so long ago, when I remembered how to smile. Already, others are reflecting my smiles and my caring. I share the candle of love and happiness gladly.

Always will I bathe my days in the golden glow of enthusiasm.

Enthusiasm is the greatest asset in the world. Its potential value far surpasses money and power and influence. Single-handed, the enthusiast convinces and dominates where the wealth accumulated by a small army of workers would scarcely raise a tremor of interest. Enthusiasm tramples over prejudice and opposition, spurns inaction, storms the citadel of its object and, like an avalanche, overwhelms and engulfs all obstacles. I have learned a great lesson—enthusiasm is my faith in action! With faith I cannot fail.

Always will I bathe my days in the golden glow of enthusiasm.

Some of us are enthusiastic at times and a few even retain their eagerness for a day or a week. All that is good but I must and I will form the habit of sustaining my enthusiasm indefinitely, honestly, and sincerely so that the success I enjoy today can be repeated tomorrow and next week and next month. Enthusiasm, the love for whatever it is I am doing at the moment, works in marvelous ways I need not even attempt to understand but I do know that it will give additional vitality to my muscles and my mind.

Enthusiasm in all I do will become, with hard work, a habit. We first must make our habits and then, good or bad, they make us. Enthusiasm will be my chariot to a better life. Already I am smiling in anticipation of the good to come.

Always will I bathe my days in the golden glow of enthusiasm.

Enthusiasm can move castles and charm brutes. It is the genius of sincerity, and truth is rarely victorious without it. Like so many others, I have conducted my life with false ideas of true rewards, believing that comfort and luxury should be my goals when all that any of us need to make us really happy is something to be enthusiastic about. Enthusiasm will benefit my future more than spring rain nourishes the wheat.

Henceforth, all my days will be different than those of the past. Never again will I consider that whatever I must do to support my existence is labor, for then I will feel the strain of necessity in my work and the hours of each day will endure for what seems an eternity. Let me, instead, forget that I must work to eat and approach the day's toil with all my energy and caring and good spirit. With these qualities I will perform far better than ever before, the hours will pass swiftly, and if this enthusiastic output continues, day after day, I am certain to become more valuable to myself and to the world.

There is no person, no occupation, no trouble that cannot be affected for the good by my attitude.

Always will I bathe my days in the golden glow of enthusiasm.

In that bright glow will I be able to see, for the first time, all the good things of life that were concealed from me during those years of futility. Just as the young lover has a finer sense and more acute vision and sees, in the object of his affection, a hundred virtues and charms invisible to all other eyes, so will I, imbued with enthusiasm, have my power of perception heightened and my vision magnified until I can see the beauty and charm others cannot discern which can compensate for large loads of drudgery, privation, hardship, and even persecution. With enthusiasm I can make the best of any situation and should I stumble now and then, as even the most talented will do on occasions, I will pick myself up and go on with my life.

Always will I bathe my days in the golden glow of enthusiasm.

What a great exhilaration I feel, knowing that I possess this great power to alter my days and my entire life with my attitude. How sorry I feel for those legions who have no knowledge that they can use this great force, a force already within them, to guide their future.

I will turn back the calendar and adopt the irresistible charm of youth with its enthusiasm bubbling like a spring of mountain water. Youth sees no darkness ahead, no trap that has no escape. It forgets that there is such a thing as failure in the world and believes that mankind has been waiting, all these centuries, for him or her to come and be the liberator of truth and energy and beauty.

Today I raise my candle on high and smile at everyone.

Always will I bathe my days in the golden glow of enthusiasm.

XII

THE FOURTH
VOW OF SUCCESS

I am the possessor of a wondrous power.

I know the secret of how to influence the thoughts and actions of others when they are in my company.

This knowledge alone, wisely used, has enabled scores of ambitious individuals to soar to great heights of fame and wealth and power throughout the ages.

Sadly, only a few are aware that they possess such a power while the vast majority have paid a terrible price, in heartbreak and misery, for their ignorance. Friends have been lost, doors were closed, opportunities have vanished, and dreams were destroyed.

Until now I have been a member of the sorry majority, constantly destroying my chances at success and happiness because I foolishly abused a power I did not even know I possessed.

Through this scroll my eyes have been opened. The secret is so simple that every child understands it and instinctively uses it to his or her benefit. We can influence others by treating them in the same manner we would like them to treat us. We are all images of each other, with the same senses, the same feelings, the same hopes, the same fears, the same faults, and the same blood. If one itches, his neighbor scratches. If another smiles, her friend responds in kind.

How ignorant I have been. I know that success cannot be achieved alone. I know that there is no such thing as a self-made man or woman. I realize, therefore, that I can never achieve my goals without the help of others and yet I can see, reflecting on my past, that my actions have kept me imprisoned behind bars of regret.

Why would anyone want to contribute to my success?

Whenever I frowned, I would meet a frown in return.

Whenever I shouted in anger, angry voices would respond.

Whenever I complained, harsh looks impaled me.

Whenever I cursed, hatred always stared back.

My own actions condemned me to the world where no one ever smiles, the world of failures. I have foolishly blamed others for my plight but now I see that the fault was mine.

At long last my eyes have been opened.

This special vow of success, I pledge to uphold for the rest of my life:

Never again will I be disagreeable to a living soul.

I will smile at friend and foe alike and make every effort to find, in him or her, a quality to praise now that I realize that the deepest yearning of human nature is the craving to be appreciated. In truth, all of us have praiseworthy features and all I need do is be certain that I am complimenting from my heart with a voice that is sincere.

To praise, to smile, to show concern for others, is as beneficial to the donor as it is the recipient of such favors. This great power that affects others so strongly will work miracles in my own life as the gratitude of others returns to me in many ways. A smile remains the most inexpensive gift I can bestow on anyone and yet its power can vanquish kingdoms. And those whom I treat kindly with words of praise will soon begin to perceive good qualities in me that they never saw before.

Never again will I be disagreeable to a living soul.

My days of whining and complaining about others have come to an end. Nothing is easier than faultfinding. No talent, no self-denial, no brains, no character are required to set up in the business of grumbling. I no longer have time for that sorry pursuit. All it will do is discolor my personality so that none will want to associate with me. That was my old life. No more.

I am so grateful for this second chance.

I have wasted years of opportunity with my frowns and scowls and angry glances when a smile and a kind word would have opened many doors and softened countless hearts who could have extended helping hands. Only now am I learning the great art of life—to improve the golden moment of opportunity and catch the good that is within our reach.

Never again will I be disagreeable to a living soul.

A smile and a handshake are, in the final resolution, a simple act of love. Life, I know now, is made up not of great sacrifices or duties but of little things in which smiles and kindnesses and small obligations, given whenever and wherever possible, are what win and preserve any heart. The best portions of one's life are the small acts of consideration and caring. Kind words produce their own image in men's souls and a beautiful image it is. They soothe and quiet and comfort the hearer. They shame him out of his sour, morose, unkind feelings. I have not, as yet, commenced to use kind words in such abundance as they ought to be used but improve I will, through practice. Who would be so foolish as not to try when one's happiness hangs in the balance?

Never again will I be disagreeable to a living soul.

I can see that in the interplay of daily life it is through little acts of watchful kindness recurring daily, and even hourly, by words, tones, gestures, and looks, that affection and admiration are won and preserved. How easy it is for one benevolent being to diffuse pleasure around him and how surely is a kind heart a fountain of gladness, making everyone in its vicinity sparkle with smiles. Each night, when I retire, I pray that I have made at least one human being a little happier or a little wiser or at least a little more content with himself or herself.

How can I fail, from this moment on, if the vow I have made on this scroll is kept so that the air that I breathe, in the future, will glow with love and good wishes?

Never again will I be disagreeable to a living soul.

XIII

THE FIFTH
VOW OF SUCCESS

*T*he sun does not always shine.
The grapes are not always ripe.

The grave diggers are not always idle and peace does not always reign.

Now, regretfully, I recognize another truth. Although I have already tasted the heady wine of success, through these scrolls, I know that I cannot expect to walk through the remainder of my days on mountain peaks. No matter how much I try, how much I persist and excel in my chosen work, there will still be days and weeks and months when everything I attempt results in frustration and failure. All of us, even the most mighty and heroic, spend too many of our days living in fear of failure. Do we possess sacks of gold and precious gems? They are not enough.

Others have more. Are we protected and safe? Safe from what? Disease? Unemployment? Robbery? Do we have many friends and a family who love us? Is friendship ever to be trusted? Will their love endure?

The fear of adversity leading to failure casts a terrible shadow on all the days of our life. Its shape and colors are varied, imaginary and real, confused and clear, temporary and permanent. Adversity terrorizes the worker struggling to keep his job, the father praying that he can feed his family, the merchant hoping he will sell his goods, the soldier leading others into battle. It tortures everyone alike, prince and pauper, sage and fool, saint and criminal. Before, I had no knowledge of how to deal with adversity and the wounds I received from my defeats were serious enough to cloud my hopes and destroy my ambition. No more! This is a new life and now I know the secret of profiting from my defeats whenever they fall upon me.

Always will I seek the seed of triumph in every adversity.

There is no better school than adversity. Every defeat, every heartbreak, every loss, contains its own seed, its own lesson on how to improve my performance the next time. Never again will I contribute to my downfall by refusing to face the truth and learn from my past mistakes. Experience is the most valuable extract of suffering and yet one of the terrible conditions of this life is that its wisdom cannot be transferred to another. All must attend their own school and for each the lessons are different. There is no other way. Adversity is always the first path to truth, however, and I am prepared to learn whatever I need to know in order to improve the condition of my life.

Always will I seek the seed of triumph in every adversity.

I am better prepared, now, to deal with any adversity. I understand, for the first time, how swiftly all deeds and events, good and bad, large and small, pass on and are no more, the works of man as well as the works of nature. All things in life are not only in a constant state of change but they are the cause of constant and infinite change in each other.

Each day I stand upon a narrow ledge. Behind me is the bottomless abyss of the past. In front is the future that will swallow everything that befalls me today. No matter what fate has in store for me I know that I will relish it or I will suffer it for only a brief, brief time. So very few understand this obvious truth while the rest allow their hopes and goals to vanish as soon as tragedy strikes.

These unfortunate people carry with them, until they die, their own bed of thorns and look to others, every day, for sympathy and attention. Adversity will never destroy the person with courage and faith. All of us are tested in the furnace of disaster and not all emerge. I will emerge. Gold can remain for a month in fiery coals without losing a grain and I am more precious than any gold.

All things shall pass.

Always will I seek the seed of triumph in every adversity.

Now I can see that adversity has many benefits, little recognized. It is the only scale on which I can weigh those who profess to be my friends and learn the truth. It is also the state in which I most easily become acquainted with my inner self and it has the wondrous ability of drawing out talents in me which in prosperous circumstances would have likely remained dormant.

Adversity is with us from birth to burial. The gem cannot be polished without friction and I cannot be perfected without trials. I admit that it has done me good to be parched by the heat and drenched by the rain of life and yet I confess that every adversity I have suffered has always been followed by my cries of anger and resentment against heaven. Why should God do such a terrible thing to me?

Why did God deprive me of one thing or another which was so important to me?

Now I know that there are no times in life when opportunity, the chance to be and do, gathers so richly about my soul as when it has to suffer cruel adversity. Then everything depends on whether I raise my head or lower it in seeking help. If I resort to mere expedients and tricks, the opportunity is forever lost and I will come out no richer nor greater, nay, perhaps harder, poorer, smaller for my pain. But, if I turn to God, and I will from now on, any time of adversity can be transformed into a triumphant turning point of my life.

Always will I seek the seed of triumph in every adversity.

Whenever I am struck down, in the future, by any terrible defeat, I will always inquire of myself, after the first pain has passed, how I can turn that adversity into good. What a great opportunity that moment might present . . . to take the bitter root I am holding and transform it into a fragrant garden of flowers!

Always will I seek the seed of triumph in every adversity.

XIV
THE SIXTH
VOW OF SUCCESS

I have cheated myself for too long.

I have given mere lip service to those who have employed me and begrudged every hour of what I considered was boring toil. Work, to me, was the sorry price I had to pay to exist because the gods had not seen fit, at my birth, to place gold in my hands and a crown on my head. What a fool I have been.

Now I know that the fruit derived from labor is the sweetest of all pleasures and while genius may commence great works, only labor will complete them.

My eyes have finally been opened through these scrolls.

How much easier my work would be if I put forth as much effort trying to improve the quality of it as I have spent in trying to find excuses for not properly attending it.

There is one towering secret of success which dwarfs all other rules. It is certain to be included in every list of affirmations on creating a better life for centuries and millenniums to come and yet most of mankind will reject it, again and again, as too difficult. Wealth, position, fame, and even elusive happiness will be mine, eventually, if I determine to render more and better service, each day, than I am being paid to render. There is another and more powerful way to remember this most difficult law of life—when one is asked to go one mile, one should willingly go two. Centuries from now, even as today, only a few will have the determination to follow this great secret of achievers and they will be the honored ones.

I commence today!

Never again will I perform any task at less than my best.

Now I know that in order to grow and flourish I must attend strictly to business and keep a little in advance of the times. Those who reach the top are the ones who are not content with doing only what is required of them. They do more. They go another mile. And another. The measurement of their recompense never enters their mind. They know that eventually they will receive their reward.

There is but one certain method of achieving one's goals and that is through hard labor, both mental and physical. If I am not willing to pay that price for distinction, I should be prepared to resign myself to a future of tears and poverty while I beat my chest in self-pity over the futility of a life void of smiles and rewards. I no longer feel sorry for myself. I have stepped off that road to nowhere.

Never again will I perform any task at less than my best.

I am not chained to my work. I am not a slave. Even if I detest the tasks I must perform, I understand that drudgery is as necessary to call out the treasures of my mind, so that I can improve my lot, as harrowing and planting are to produce results for those tilling the soil. I can grow beyond any task assigned to me now, providing I never forget that I am a child of God, born to victory.

Whatever my job may be, let me perform it with love and I will not fail.

My share of the work of this day may be limited, but the fact that it is work makes it precious. The world is moved not only by the mighty muscles of our heroes but also by the aggregate of the tiny pushes of each honest worker. The secret of the true love of work is the hope of success in that work, not for the money reward, not for the time spent or for the skill exercised, but for the pride and satisfaction in the accomplishment of the work itself.

A sufficient reward for a thing well done is to have done it.

Never again will I perform any task at less than my best.

Henceforth, when my day's work has ended, I will surprise the world. I will remain at my task, just a little longer, and let that extra effort be an investment in my tomorrow. With such an attitude, so rare in this selfish world we inhabit, I cannot fail.

And yet, if I labor in such a manner, if I persist in traveling the extra mile, I must prepare myself for jeers from those who never contribute a fair day's work. In order to accomplish some great thing in this short life I realize that I must apply myself to work with such a concentration of my mind and my muscle and my time that, to those who live in the squalor of idleness, I may appear to have given leave of my senses. So be it.

Never again will I perform any task at less than my best.

Give me love and work, these two only, and I will be able to live a contented life.

I could not long be happy without food or drink or clothes or shelter but I may have all these things to perfection and still be unhappy. What is the best thing for a river? It is to keep moving. If it stops, it stagnates. The best thing for me is that which keeps my currents flowing. Few people realize how much of their happiness is dependent upon their work, upon the fact that they are kept busy and not left to feed upon themselves. I am nothing without my work. The prime secret of happiness is something to do.

Never again will I perform any task at less than my best.

Never again will I fail to go the extra mile or render less than my pay deserves.

I will do my work, henceforth, with all the intensity I can put forth—not just my work and no more, but a little more, that little more which in time will be worth all the rest. And if I suffer, as I often will, and if I doubt the value of my efforts, as I must on occasions, I will still do my work. I will put my heart into it and the sky will clear and from out of the very doubt and suffering will be born the supreme joy of life.

Let me always obey this special vow of success:

Never again will I perform any task at less than my best.

XV

THE SEVENTH
VOW OF SUCCESS

I have scattered my efforts in so many directions.

I have wasted so many seasons running from one rainbow to the next.

I have spent countless years letting empty buckets down into empty wells.

Success, happiness, wealth, I continued to hope, would someday be mine.

I waited in vain. Without the miracle of these scrolls I might have waited forever. How sad. On the street of by and by, one eventually arrives at the house of never.

All that is now behind me.

Now I understand why success has eluded me. The person who is perpetually hesitating between which of two things he or she will do, will do neither. If I waver from plan to plan, from goal to goal, and constantly bend in the wind, like a lily, to every point in the compass, I will never accomplish anything great or useful.

It is those who concentrate on but one thing at a time who advance in this world. The great man or woman is the one who never steps outside his or her specialty or foolishly dissipates his or her individuality. Now I know the great secret that was always before my eyes and yet I was too blind to see.

Always will I throw my whole self into the task at hand.

The great difference between those who succeed and those who fail does not consist in the amount of work done by each but in the amount of intelligent work. Many of those who fail most ignominiously do enough to achieve grand success but they labor haphazardly at whatever they are assigned, building up with one hand to tear down with the other. They do not grasp circumstances and change them into opportunities. They have no faculty for turning honest defeats into telling victories. With ability enough and ample time, the major ingredients of success, they are forever throwing back and forth an empty shuttle and the real web of their life is never woven.

Never again will I only lay my hands on

my work when I should have committed my entire being. My eyes are open at last. I will do whatever I am doing, henceforth, as if there were nothing else in the world of any importance.

The creation of a thousand forests is in a single acorn.

Concentration and perseverance built the great pyramids on Egypt's plains.

The master of a single trade can support a family. The master of seven trades cannot support himself. The wind is never for the sailor who knows not to what port he is bound. Now I know where I want to go and I know how to reach my destination.

Always will I throw my whole self into the task at hand.

Not many things indifferently, but one thing supremely, is the demand of our world. He who scatters his efforts cannot hope to succeed.

If a salamander be cut in two, the front half will run forward and the other backward. Such is the progress of he who divides his purpose. Success is always jealous of scattered energies.

I am prepared for great changes in my life. The world will know I have changed course. What an immense power over life is the power of possessing direct aims. My voice, my dress, my look, my very motions and gestures will change as I begin to live my days with a purpose.

How could I, like so many others, have remained blind to this great truth?

The person who knows one thing and does it better than anyone else, even if it only be the art of raising lentils, receives the crown he merits. If he raises the best lentils by having concentrated all his energy to that end, he is a benefactor of mankind and is rewarded as such.

Always will I throw my whole self into the task at hand.

I will decide on my goals and keep them forever in my thoughts. We find only what we seek with all our heart. If I look for nothing in particular from life, I will find just that. The bee is not the only insect that visits the rose but it is the only one that carries honey away. It matters not how rich the materials we have gleaned from the years of our study and the toil in our youth. If we go out into life with no well-defined idea of our future work we can be certain that there will be no happy and accidental circumstance that will arrange what we do into an imposing structure with magnificent proportions.

We are often told to aim high in life but we must aim at what we would hit, instead.

A general purpose is not enough. The arrow shot from the bow does not wander around to see what it can hit on its way, but flies straight to the mark.

The widely dispersed explosion of thunder produces no results compared to a single, concentrated bolt of lightning.

Now I know that I cannot pursue a worthy goal, steadily and persistently, with all the powers of my mind and yet fail. If I focus the rays of sun with a burning glass, even in the coldest days of winter, I can kindle a fire with ease.

Always will I throw my whole self into the task at hand.

The weakest living creature, by concentrating his powers on a single object, can accomplish good results while the strongest, by dispersing his effort over many chores, may fail to accomplish anything. Drops of water, by continually falling, hone their passage through the hardest of rocks but the hasty torrent rushes over it with hideous uproar and leaves no trace behind.

I will leave my traces. The world will know I have been here.

Always will I throw my whole self into the task at hand.

XVI

THE EIGHTH
VOW OF SUCCESS

I have been so blind.

Never once did I recognize opportunity when it presented itself in my life because always it has been disguised as hard work.

Never once did I take notice of that golden chariot waiting to transport me to a better life since my eyes were always filled with tears of self-pity as I wandered along the back roads of life with no destination.

My vision is no longer impaired by my attitude because my attitude has been transformed.

Now I understand that opportunities never appear with their potential for wealth or success or honor painted upon them. Every task I do must be accomplished with my very best effort or I risk having the greatest of opportunities slip away from me without the sound of a warning bell. A day dawns, quite like all other days, and in it a single hour blossoms, just like all other hours, but it is possible that in that day and that hour I may be confronted with the chance of a lifetime. To face every task, no matter how difficult and menial it may be, with courage and persistence, is the only way I can be certain of seizing the supreme opportunities when they come, whether they have been proclaimed with fanfare or are hiding, as usual, beneath a mantle of dust.

The old me, despising each day's labor and venting my frustrations on everyone I touched, could never have been capable of committing myself to lay siege to opportunity. Now, through these scrolls, I am rebuilding my life and henceforth I will go forward with head held high, searching for opportunity as fiercely as the starving lion searches for food.

Never again will I wait and hope for opportunity to embrace me.

I have turned my back on the past. None of those failures will slow my new stride toward that bright land of success and happiness where I will spend the rest of my life. Now I know that if I want to sing I can always find a song.

I look back now only to reminisce. What a sorry failure I had allowed myself to become. There is an old proverb which says, "Enjoy the little you have while the fool is hunting for more." That was what I believed and how I acted, in the past, for do not all old proverbs speak the truth? No! I am beginning a new life and I have reversed that proverb just as I have altered the actions of my past life. Now that proverb reads, "While the fool is enjoying the little he has, I will hunt for more!"

Never again will I wait and hope for opportunity to embrace me.

I have already improved, in these few weeks, many qualities in my character so that I am now better equipped to recognize opportunity and claim my share. Already I have rooted out vile habits that held me back, through daily repeating of the words on these scrolls, and the reconstruction has only begun. Let me start where I am, even with some qualities still within me that often made me despise myself. Let me attend to them, one at a time, and use God's strength to assist my weaknesses. At the very least I will be better than I am if I have the courage to reach beyond my grasp and faith enough to believe I can be what I ought to be.

In the past I have foolishly allowed my

failures and regrets to so weigh me down that I have had to travel always with my head bowed low and my eyes on the ground. Now that my heavy load of the past has been tossed aside and my vision has been elevated I can see, everywhere that I look, open doors welcoming me to a better life.

Never again will I wait and hope for opportunity to embrace me.

Every day when I post my goals, I will list, at the very top, a reminder that I should remain alert to opportunities. And each morning, when I awake, I will go forth to meet the day with a smile, no matter what unpleasant tasks confront me. Opportunity, like love, is never attracted by gloom and despair. Now I know that those who succeed best in life are always cheerful and hopeful people who go about their work with a smile on their face and take the chances and changes of this mortal life with humor and good cheer, facing rough and smooth alike as it comes. These are the wise men and women who always make more opportunities than they find.

How could I have lived so many years without perceiving the truth that now is so clear to me? Why is it that so many of us see the golden moments in the stream of life rush past us and we recognize nothing but sand? Why do the angels come to visit us and we only know them after they are gone?

Opportunities, many times, are so small that we glimpse them not and yet they are often the seeds of great enterprises. Opportunities are also everywhere and so I must always let my hook be hanging. When I least expect it, a great fish will swim by.

Never again will I wait and hope for opportunity to embrace me.

I am not the person I was only a few weeks ago.

Opportunities will never remain concealed from me again.

No longer do I wail and tear my clothes and curse at the world for my lack of the good things in life. I am still discontented with my lot but now it is a discontent that stands in the rain and searches the heavens for the blue sky and stars. There are two kinds of discontented in this world, the discontented that works and the discontented that wrings its hands. The first gets what it wants and the second loses what it has. There is no cure for the first but success and there is no cure at all for the second. I know who I am. I like who I am. Thank you, God.

Now I understand that opportunity knocks

at no door. She will answer only when I knock. I will knock often and loud.

Never again will I wait and hope for opportunity to embrace me.

XVII

THE NINTH
VOW OF SUCCESS

I have been too easy on myself.

I have closed the book on each day much too swiftly.

Never have I taken the time, before retiring, to tally the cost of both the good and the bad that I have brought upon myself during the day.

Never have I dared to review, with courage and honesty, my thoughts and words and actions of one day in order to better shape the next.

The truth about success and how to achieve it has never been hidden from me. I have just been so caught up in the struggle to survive that I failed to recognize it.

At the completion of each day, I was done with it. Any blunders or failures or accidents that darkened my hours were quickly excused away. Tomorrow is a new day, I would promise myself. Perhaps life would be kinder to me. Wrong!

At last my vision is in focus.

Now I can see that the world is a market where everything is marked at a set price and I must stand by my decision, whatever I buy with my time, labor, and ingenuity, whether it be riches, ease, fame, integrity, or knowledge. I must never act like a child who, when he has purchased one thing, regrets that he does not possess another. Since the daily trades that I make for part of my life are difficult to rescind, let me be certain in the future that I am laying up things of value and permanence for my toil and sweat. The only way that can be done, with certainty, is for me to perform a special exercise, daily, before I surrender to sleep.

Always will I examine, each night, my deeds of the fading day.

The very worst of my vices and bad habits will abate of themselves if they are brought to an accounting every day. What a joy, what a blessed sleep will always follow such a personal inspection.

Questions form in my head with little prompting:

What infirmity have I mastered today?

What passion opposed?

What temptation resisted?

What virtue acquired?

Through these scrolls I have already commenced to greet each new day with a plan so that the high road upon which I travel is marked well. Now, at day's end, I will carefully weigh the progress and the problems of my journey and this latest of my acquired good habits will create, in my mind, a diary of today and a textbook for tomorrow.

Always will I examine, each night, my deeds of the fading day.

In the evening, as soon as my candle is extinguished, I will review the words and actions of every hour of the day and I will allow nothing to escape my examination for why should I fear the sight of my errors when I have the power to admonish and forgive myself?

Perhaps I was a little too cutting in a certain dispute. My opinion might well have been withheld for it stung but did no good. The thing was true but all truths are not to be spoken at all times. I should have held my tongue for there is no contending, either with fools or with our superiors. I have done ill but it shall be so no more.

Experience is the name that mankind has always given to its follies or its sorrows. It need not be so. Today's lessons can be tomorrow's foundation for a better life providing I have the will to learn from them and I do.

Always will I examine, each night, my deeds of the fading day.

Let me review my actions, let me observe myself as my greatest enemy might do and I will become my own best friend. I will begin, right now, to become what I will be hereafter. Darkness may fall but sleep will not cloud my eyes until I have reviewed, in full, the events of my day.

What have I left undone which ought to be done?

What have I done which could have been done better?

One of the great undiscovered joys of this life comes from doing everything one attempts to the best of one's ability. There is a special sense of satisfaction, a pride in surveying such a work, a work which is rounded, full, exact, complete in all its parts, which the superficial person who leaves his or her work in a slovenly, slipshod, half-finished condition, can never know. It is this conscientious completeness which turns any work into art. The smallest task, well done, becomes a miracle of achievement.

Today's work will be surpassed tomorrow. It cannot be otherwise. Improvement forever follows examination and review. Everyone should be wiser today than yesterday.

Always will I examine, each night, my deeds of the fading day.

Did I survive the day without pitying myself?

Did I greet the dawn with a map and a goal?

Was I pleasant and agreeable to all I met?

Did I attempt to go the extra mile?

Did I remain alert for opportunities?

Did I search for the good in every problem?

Did I smile in the faces of anger and hatred?

Did I concentrate my strength and purpose?

What can be more profitable than this daily review of my life so that I can live it with pride and satisfaction?

No longer will my day end when the sun sets. There is now, one more act to perform.

Always will I examine, each night, my deeds of the fading day.

XVIII

THE FINAL VOW

I promise . . .

I swear . . .

I vow . . . to never forget that the greatest talent God has bestowed on me is the power to pray. Through triumph and despair, love and heartbreak, ecstasy and pain, applause and rejection, success and failure, I can always light up the lamp of faith in my heart with a prayer and it will lead me safely through the mists of doubt, the black darkness of futility, the narrow, thorny ways of sickness and sorrow, and over the treacherous places of temptation.

Now I know that God will hear only what my heart speaks.

In the morning, prayer is the key that will open to me the treasures of God's blessings and in the evening it is the key that places me under his protection.

So long as it is possible to pray, there is always hope and courage. Without prayer I can do little; with it all things are possible. Let this tenth and final vow forever guide me in the conduct of my life:

Always will I maintain contact, through prayer, with my creator.

The fewer words, the better prayer.

Among my prayers will be these simple words. . .

Prayer to an Unseen Friend

My special Friend, thank You for listening to me. You know how hard I am trying to fulfill Your faith in me.

Thank You, also, for this place in which I dwell. Let neither work nor play, no matter how satisfying or glorious, ever separate me, for long, from the love that unites my precious family.

Teach me how to play the game of life with fairness, courage, fortitude, and confidence.

Provide me with a few friends who understand me and yet remain my friends.

Allow me a forgiving heart and a mind unafraid to travel even though the trail may not be marked.

Give me a sense of humor and a little leisure with nothing to do.

Help me to strive for the highest legitimate reward of merit, ambition, and opportunity, and yet never allow me to forget to extend a kindly, helping hand to others who need encouragement and assistance.

Provide me with the strength to encounter whatever is to come, that I be brave in peril, constant in tribulation, temperate in anger, and always prepared for any change of fortune.

Enable me to give a smile instead of a frown, a cheerful kindly word instead of harshness and bitterness.

Make me sympathetic to the grief of others, realizing that there are hidden woes in every life, no matter how exalted.

Keep me forever serene in every activity of life, neither unduly boastful nor given to the more serious sin of self-depreciation.

In sorrow, may my soul be uplifted by the thought that if there were no shadow, there would be no sunshine.

In failure, preserve my faith.

In success, keep me humble.

Steady me to do the full share of my work, and more, as well as I can, and when that is done, stop me, pay what wages Thou wilt, and permit me to say, from a loving heart . . . a grateful Amen.

XIX

*E*rasmus was seated on a wooden bench, near the courtyard's huge fountain, his elbows resting on his knees. He continued to stare down at his sandals even after he heard footsteps approaching.

"What is wrong, Erasmus?" Galenus asked uncertainly.

"How long has he been alone on that mountain?"

Galenus smiled. It was the same question he had heard, many times each day, for the past week. "Twenty-eight days have now passed since we parted company with Hafid."

Erasmus shook his head despondently and stood. "Please walk with me, Galenus. Your companionship and smiling face have been priceless assets during these worry-filled days."

Soon they were on the north side of the landscaped patio and standing beneath the arcade of cypress trees that sheltered Lisha's tomb. Erasmus nodded toward the nearby mahogany bench and said, "Every morning, when Hafid is home, he always sits there and talks to his Lisha as if she were nearby, picking flowers. Then he naps. The only thing he disliked about his speaking tours, he often said, was that he missed conversing with his lady every day."

"In all my strolls I have never ventured into this part of the courtyard," said the promoter as he continued walking toward the raised marble vault while Erasmus rested on Hafid's favorite bench.

"What an unusual rose!" exclaimed Galenus, suddenly kneeling before the thorny green bush that guarded the single bronze door of the tomb.

"What can be so unusual about a white rose?" Erasmus sighed. "It is there because it was Lisha's favorite. When Hafid is finally entombed, next to her, he has requested that we plant a red rose close to Lisha's white one."

"Erasmus!" Galenus cried out. "You must come here! Now!"

Startled by the urgency in his guest's voice, the old bookkeeper leaped up and hurried toward Galenus who was sitting on the ground, mouth ajar, his trembling hand pointing toward a double rose in full bloom.

"Look, Erasmus!"

Clusters of white roses, both in bud and bloom, nearly covered the tall plant but Galenus was pointing to only one rose.

"It cannot be," sobbed Erasmus, falling to his knees. "It cannot be!"

"But it is," shouted Galenus as he stared in disbelief. "A lovely red rose growing on a white rosebush!"

"Something has happened to Hafid," moaned Erasmus. "We must go to him. Now!"

In less than an hour, a small carriage raced out of the palace stables and by noon, with Galenus at the reins, they had reached the base of Mount Hermon. Soon after they had commenced their climb, Erasmus consulted his map and directed Galenus to the right when they arrived at a three-pronged fork in the dirt road. Later, they passed the giant column of stone and Erasmus said, "We should be there very soon. His small retreat, Sergius once told me, is secluded in a grove of trees."

"There it is," shouted Galenus, waving his whip toward the stand of junipers surrounded by white rocks and drifting sand. As soon as they entered the grove, Galenus brought the wagon to a stop. Only a few cubits ahead stood Hafid's wagon with its reins tossed over a thick post near the front of the small house.

"Apparently he is preparing to return to Damascus," said Erasmus as he and Galenus stepped from their wagon. "Hafid has probably completed his task, at last, and is coming home. It appears that our worries and this trip were in vain."

Galenus knocked on the front door several times but there was no response. He turned toward Erasmus who, without hesitation, slowly pushed open the door and called out, "Hafid! Hafid! This is Erasmus. Answer me, please!"

There was no response. As soon as they were inside, Erasmus saw the large writing table with its quills and bottles of ink. On the table was another familiar object. "Look, there is the old chest that Hafid purchased in Rome!"

The chest was open and filled to the top with scrolls. "Galenus, see how these scrolls have been numbered on the outside of each skin by Hafid. That is exactly how the other scrolls, that he received so long ago, were marked. If I did not know better, I would swear that I was looking at the original chest and scrolls that Pathros passed on to my master when he was only a camel boy. This is, indeed, a day of miracles."

Erasmus reached into the chest, removed the scroll marked with the Roman numeral "X," untied the small green ribbon, and slowly unrolled the parchment.

"Thanks be to God," he said, smiling as he turned the parchment so that Galenus could see Hafid's writing. "The master has completed his mission. This is the final scroll. Now, let us find the man so that we can all go home. He cannot be far."

Shouting his name, they went out the front door and slowly worked their way around to the rear where they could see the circle of white boulders for the first time.

"There he is," shouted Erasmus, "leaning

against the largest boulder! Praise be to God. Hafid! Hafid!"

Erasmus could not move as swiftly as his younger companion. By the time he had arrived at the boulder, Galenus had already arisen from his kneeling position with both hands upraised. Tears were flowing down his cheeks and he sobbed, "Erasmus, our friend is dead. Hafid is finally with his beloved Lisha."

Erasmus moaned and fell to the ground, cradling the lifeless form of his master against his chest. "The body is still warm. Had we arrived earlier we might have saved him. He died alone. That is not right. He died alone. Oh, Hafid, please forgive me. Have mercy on me for not taking better care of thee. I love you. I'm so sorry that you had to die alone."

A warm breeze suddenly blew across the mountain. Galenus knelt near Erasmus and said, "Dry your tears, old bookkeeper. Your master did not die alone."

"What do you mean?" cried Erasmus as he continued to stroke Hafid's forehead gently.

"He did not die alone," repeated Galenus. "Look!"

In their deep sorrow and shock, neither had noticed that wrapped around the shoulders of the greatest salesman in the world was a red robe . . . a frayed red robe.

ABOUT THE AUTHOR

OG MANDINO is the most widely read inspirational and self-help author in the world. His thirteen books have sold more than eighteen million copies in seventeen languages. He is also a member of the International Speakers Hall of Fame and one of the most sought-after speakers in the nation. Countless thousands the world over have acknowledged in their letters the great debt they owe Og Mandino for the miracle his words have wrought in their lives. His beloved masterpieces include *The Greatest Salesman in the World, The Greatest Secret in the World, The Greatest Success in the World, The Greatest Miracle in the World, The Gift of Acabar, The Christ Commission, Og Mandino's University of Success, The Choice, Mission: Success!,* and *A Better Way to Live.*